Wax Plant

Plants and Flowers
to Decorate Your Home

Plants and Flowers to Decorate Your Home

by Julilly H. Kohler

Photographs by Bill Helms
Drawings by Grambs Miller

 Golden Press • New York

Western Publishing Company, Inc., Racine, Wisconsin

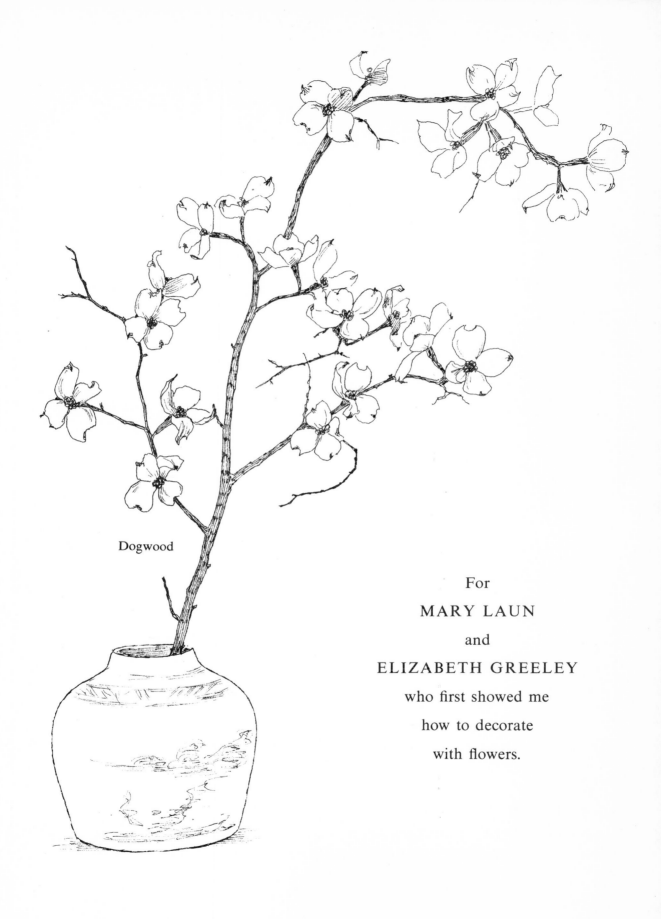

Dogwood

For

MARY LAUN

and

ELIZABETH GREELEY

who first showed me

how to decorate

with flowers.

Contents

Philodendron
(Philodendron selloum)

Ivy

The Joy of Decorating with Plants and Flowers

INTERIOR DECORATING is a term that many people associate with slick magazines, icy receptions in antique shops, and Italian silk brocades at forty dollars a yard. Actually it is no more than a simple description of the effort to make the inside of a home as attractive as possible. It doesn't always require expensive materials. Flowers, greens, plants, and vines can bring beauty into every room in your home, and they are probably some of the most effective decorating devices you will ever find. All you need to know are the varieties that are available, a few hints for prolonging their life indoors, and how and where to use them to the best advantage. You will also want to know a few basic rules for arranging flowers and greens, but you don't always have to follow the rules. The more you experiment, the more you will learn—and the more you will enjoy your own creations.

You need never hesitate to learn from all possible sources: the professionals who lecture or give demonstrations of their individual styles, the arrangements in flower shows and house-and-garden tours, the photographs in magazines, even the charming decorative achievements of your friends. If you see an effect that is good, try it yourself with a slightly different flower or green or container or accessory. You don't mind using friends' recipes for unusual dishes, so there is no reason to be shy about copying flower arrangements that particularly please you.

Where can you use flowers and plants to decorate your home? Look around you. A brass pot of zinnias on the coffee table that echoes the print in your curtains will do wonders in your living room. The dark corner of your family room will come alive when you brighten it with a handsome container of tall *Philodendron selloum.* Do you have an entry hall? That would be a perfect spot for a bowl of geraniums or chrysanthemums to welcome guests and (not incidentally) your family. How about the fireplace in the summertime when it's the season for cooling, not heating? A decorative pleated paper fan spread across the empty andirons as a background for potted green jade plants or dieffenbachias or English ivy will give the room a fresh focus.

And potted plants can do more than dress up the fireplace or brighten a dark corner. They can serve as architectural helps as well. Try using them as a divider between the living and dining areas of a room. In a small apartment, a group of tall and medium-size plants can form an attractive "wall" between kitchen and breakfast room.

Consider the decor and the texture of the materials in a room before you select the flowers to decorate it. In a country home with casual furniture and cotton, denim, or printed slipcovers or curtains, choose country or casual flowers—marigolds, daisies, bachelor-buttons, cosmos, zinnias—the possibilities are unlimited. If you prefer a more formal, eighteenth-century look, choose snapdragons, petunias, roses, or carnations to complement the colors of the draperies or to create the atmosphere that reflects your taste.

Sometimes a bedroom is lacking in color or needs a balancing color accent. The plain curtained windows don't give the effect you had hoped for. Plants can solve your problem perfectly. If you have a sunny windowsill—sunny for at least half the day—use it for plants that will add the color you need. Try charming dwarf geraniums, each with different-colored leaves and flowers. A collection of African violets will bloom well on east or north windows without bright sunshine. Unusual foliage plants in white pots

may add the accent the room needs. Or small pots of blooming cyclamen or azaleas in pink, red, or white can be slipped into plastic pots that will blend or contrast with the color of the woodwork of the window. Plastic containers are as good for plants as clay pots. If the green or yellow or bittersweet colors you find in a garden shop don't match your pale pink window, buy white plastic pots and a little spray can of pale pink paint. In five minutes, back at home, you can transform the white pots to pale pink pots, the exact color you were seeking.

On the kitchen window, a row of herb plants that you can grow from seed or buy in 3-inch pots are not only decorative but are also ready when you need them in gourmet dishes.

There are several varieties of plants in hanging baskets—*Browallia speciosa major,* lovely blue or white; trailing geraniums, English ivy, wandering Jew, spider plants—that will add interest and beauty to any window in the house. On the sun porch, fill an attractive wheeled cart with blooming fibrous begonias. Brighten the dining room with an indoor window box of impatiens. In any room, a pot of blooming narcissuses, hyacinths, or tulips (which you have potted yourself in October) can welcome spring two months early.

These are only a few examples of the many places in your home where fresh flowers and plants can add a "decorator" touch.

And, of course, there are always times when you will want to glamorize your home for a dinner party, a luncheon, a birthday party, a Derby party, an Election Day party. Perhaps you've decided to set aside a little extra money to spend on an arrangement from the florist for these occasions. But at the end of the month you find that the bill that covers his services is certainly more than a "little extra." Why not learn how to make the arrangements yourself?

If you take a little time to learn how to grow—or buy—and handle flowers, greens, potted plants, shrubs, and vines so that they take their proper place in home decorating, you will discover that you are not only saving money, but enriching your way of life as well. Think of flowers when you think of the special days in your life that you love to celebrate—births, christenings, marriages, graduations—all the moments you treasure. And each changing season deserves consideration. Pussy-willow branches stir the heart with the awareness of spring; orange and gold leaves and flowers bring the glowing colors of Indian summer indoors in October. Think ahead. What can you do to bring the outdoors indoors at any season of the year? Plot it out in your mind; use your imagination.

Sometimes a simple, original, creative touch will give you greater satisfaction and be more effective than any arrangement you find in a book or magazine. There are always unexpected places for an impromptu arrangement. In the kitchen, where so many hours are spent, one spray of fragrant lilac blossoms in a child's battered mug can brighten the day. When guests come in for a glass of cold beer after a tennis game, how wonderful to see that your husband has picked a silly pink petunia and put it on the tray in a brown beer bottle, in honor of the champion! In the powder room a small bowl of seasonal flowers adds a delightful touch. Even your front door can always say "Welcome" with a May basket, or a Halloween concoction of Indian corn and bittersweet, or some Christmas greens.

Don't worry. You can do it. You've begun already.

African Violets

A Quick Review of Flowers, Shrubs, Vines, and Herbs

ONE GOOD WAY to begin decorating your home with living flowers or shrubs is to review the materials that are available. This could depend upon where you live. The United States is subject to every kind of climate from glacial to tropical, and is divided into nine "hardiness zones" according to temperature. A zone map, published by the U.S. Department of Agriculture, is reproduced on page 104 to help you decide which zone you live in. In between the two oceans the zones grow colder as they go north, but sometimes you can be fooled by the mountains or the Great Lakes. That's why northern Ohio is colder than southern Nebraska! Which means that if you have a "green thumb," or hope to cultivate one, you will have to check to see if the climate is right for the flowers and shrubs you want to plant before you buy them. On pages 106–142 of this book, you will find charts listing the common and horticultural names of the most popular flowers, vines, shrubs and plants that you might choose for decorating your home. They show the zones in which each plant will grow, its average height, its range of colors, when it blooms, whether it is easy or hard to grow, when to cut or buy it, and how to condition flowers and plants you want to use in arrangements. If you are not interested in growing the plants, the chart will suggest where you can buy them.

Are you on a seed-catalogue list? Send for every catalogue you read about. They are full of fascinating pictures and are almost as useful as a course in horticulture. It's an easy way to learn the names of flowers and a great opportunity to see them in color.

Whether you grow or buy the flowers and greens you use in decorating, you may find it helpful to review the basic divisions of live plant material. All the flowers, shrubs, and vines mentioned on the following pages are good material for home decorating.

Flowers

Flowers can be divided into groups in accordance with their habits of living and blooming. *Annuals*—which last only one season, bloom lavishly and die with the first frost—supply brilliant flowers for one summer. You probably know most of these: Ageratums, Coxcomb, Cosmos, Dahlias, from seed, Marigolds, Petunias, Salvia ('Blue Bedder'), Salvia ('Evening Glow'), Snapdragons and Zinnias.

Dahlias are usually listed as tubers and are planted in late spring and dug up and stored after their summer bloom. But tubers must begin as seeds, and since 1960, when Unwin dwarf dahlia seeds were offered on the market, many home gardeners have planted dahlia seeds and treated these plants as annuals.

Of course, these are only a few of the available annuals. They must be planted each spring, and under favorable conditions

Zinnia

they set their own seed before fall comes. Some, like marigolds, petunias, and zinnias, will grow in the tropical zones happily all fall, winter, and spring, until the summer sun dries them up.

Dahlia

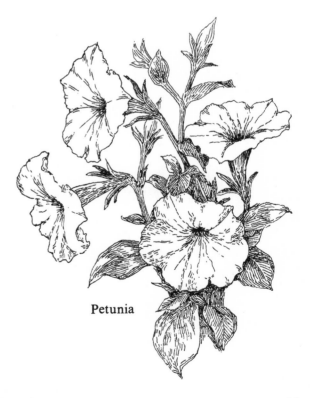

Petunia

English Daisy

Forget-me-not

discarded after blooming is over, but if kept, mature seeds in fall before they succumb to the frost. They do not do well farther south than Zone 7.

Daylily

Some flowers take two seasons to bloom and, after blooming, die. They are the *biennials*. Biennials and plants grown as such include forget-me-nots, English daisies, pansies, and hollyhocks, among many others. Their seeds are planted in summer. They grow until the fall and rest in winter, then bloom in heartwarming splendor the following spring or summer. Usually they are

The third group of flowers is called *perennials* because, once seeded and transplanted, they will live many years. When frost comes

Hollyhock

Iris

in the fall their greens and stems shrivel, but their roots are safely buried and protected from the cold and ready to send up fresh green shoots the following spring.

Gerbera

Perennials you probably know and will use include phlox, delphiniums, daylilies, iris, chrysanthemums, peonies, and many more. Three familiar flowers that are treated as annuals in the North can live sturdily in Zones 8 and 9 as perennials; they are poinsettias, geraniums, and salvias *(Salvia farinacea* and *Salvia splendens)*. Three charming ones that can live only in the Tropics and along the West Coast are carnations, gerberas, and lantanas.

Lantana

In addition to the flowers that come from seed or rooted stock are the beauties that bloom from bulbs, such as crocuses, narcissuses, tulips, and scillas. If planted outdoors, they last many years. Indoors they can be forced to bloom early to suit your own calendar. Besides the spring bulbs, there are summer flowers that grow from tubers or corms: tuberous-rooted begonias, dahlias, gladioluses, cannas. Except in tropical climates, these tubers and corms are planted in early summer and taken up just before frost; but they, like the spring bulbs, increase each year and last many seasons.

Gladiolus

Finally, there are lilies, which are also grown from bulbs and furnish marvelous flowers from May till October in almost every state in the union. They must be planted in late fall or early spring or forced in greenhouses; but their color, form, and long life make them one of the most desirable flowers.

13

Shrubs

Some shrubs are almost treelike in size —some are evergreen—some have blossoms that are seasonal, and some bloom all year round in tropical climates. The flowering shrubs are especially lovely for decorating your home. If you live in Massachusetts or Connecticut you will know the thrill of seeing the broad-leaved evergreen rhododendron bloom in June—white, pink, lavender, deep rose. If you reside in Memphis, Tennessee, or Vicksburg, Mississippi, you will have your favorite blooming azalea without which you feel you couldn't live in March or April. Yet in Wisconsin and Minnesota these beauties cannot withstand the winter days when the thermometer registers an unbelievable 29 degrees below zero. (Neither can the human inhabitants sometimes!) There they welcome spring with yellow forsythia, white bridal wreath, and lilac. In Kentucky and Alabama and the Carolinas the breathtaking dogwood and redbud, both actually small native trees, turn the countryside into a paradise. Farther south, camellias are the reigning beauties; and in the West, from Oregon to Arizona, weigelia, holly, and pyracantha grow in abundance, and citrus fruits, hibiscus, and oleander flourish in tropical California and Florida. All these flowering shrubs or trees will bring beauty and color to your arrangements.

EVERGREENS

This special class of shrubs, whether broad-leaved or needled, can be found in all parts of this country. Without flowers, they are beautiful in shape and color and will last weeks, sometimes months, in your home. Here are some evergreen shrubs that are usually available:

Arborvitae *(Thuja):* rich dark green, with scalelike leaves arranged in broad fans which

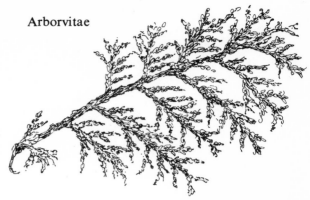

Arborvitae

hang irregularly on the twigs. Most widely grown evergreen in America. Good for Christmas decorations and wreaths. Zone 2.

Boxwood

Boxwood *(Buxus sempervirens):* the pride of Virginia, Maryland, and the Carolinas. Deep, glossy green leaves are small and oval. Fresh, delightful odor, long lasting. Zone 6. Hardy to Lancaster, York, and Bethlehem, Pennsylvania, and Nantucket Island.

American Holly

Holly, American *(Ilex opaca):* leaf dull green above, pale below. Spiny teeth on margin. Red berries. Zone 5.

English Holly

Holly, English *(Ilex aquifolium):* leaf glossy rich green. Thorns. Red berries mostly in clusters. Shrub or tree. Hardy from Zone 5 south along the coast, as well as in Missouri, Texas, and Oregon. Hundreds of varieties including variegated-leaved sorts. Beautiful for Christmas decoration. If you're lucky you can grow two in your yard; male and female plants are necessary to produce the berries.

Juniper

Juniper: pale green to blue-green or blue, with leaves sometimes needlelike, sometimes scalelike. Berrylike fruits. Easiest to grow, from Zone 2 southward.

Magnolia *(M. grandiflora):* an evergreen that is really a tree, the aristocrat of the South. Not hardy north of Zone 5. Also called Bull Bay. Leaves are oblong, 5–9 inches long, shining green above, rusty-woolly beneath. The stems are large and, if cut slantwise, will last weeks in water. If put into glycerine to be preserved, the leaves

will turn a handsome brown and will last forever (see page 93). They can be ordered from the florist unless you have friends who will cut some for you from their tree.

Magnolia

Mountain laurel, rhododendron: broad-leaved, evergreen shrubs. Without their blossoms, they provide handsome foliage year round.

The evergreen shrub, mountain laurel *(Kalmia latifolia),* hardy from Zone 3 southward, is native to this country. From New England to North Carolina its showy pink and white blossoms grow wild or cultivated in May and June. If you can't grow it in your zone, it can be found at your florist. Its leaves are narrowly oval, 2–4 inches long, tough and leathery. It lasts for weeks and looks attractive alone or with other flowers.

Mountain Laurel

15

Rhododendron

unchanged throughout the year. The needles taper, the fruit is bright scarlet, berrylike, about ½ inch long. The English yew *(T. baccata)* is not as hardy as the Japanese *(T. cuspidata)* which lives from Zone 3 southward. Yews will take shade or sun, and greens last for weeks when used in an arrangement.

NONFLOWERING GREENS

Some shrubs that are not evergreen make charming decorations.

The rhododendron has leaves 3–5 inches long, shining green on top, paler beneath. It will grow near the coast from Zone 4 to Zone 5 or 6 if it's not in hot, windy plains. The finest rhododendrons in America today are grown in the Pacific Northwest. Lucky you, if you have some shrubs in your yard. Otherwise they can be ordered from the florist.

Dwarf Huckleberry

Huckleberry *(Gaylussacia baccata):* erect, bright green small leaf with tooth edges; inexpensive filler which you can find at your florist.

Yew

Winged Euonymus

Yew *(Taxus):* the most widely planted popular evergreen for use as specimen trees or shrubs, accent plants or hedges. Yews have rich, dark green foliage that remains

Winged euonymus *(Euonymus alatus):* green in spring and a marvelous rosy red in autumn with strange winged bark on its branches.

Ideas for Spring

*Suddenly it's spring! Trees, land, and streams provide buds
and flowers to decorate the earth. Which are your favorites?
This lovely house is deep in the woods at the edge of Lake Michigan.
The centerpiece is made of marsh marigolds and pale blue
forget-me-nots. White lilacs rise from a container on a plastic
rectangle. The macramé basket holds wax plant (Hoya carnosa).*

ABOVE: *Terrace-living room. A glorious setting built all around the east end of the house. Trees seem to be growing up through it. Handsome enameled aluminum furniture with big glass-topped table set for coffee and dessert. Flower arrangement of tulips and lilacs. Two hanging baskets of pink and white fuchsias. Background arrangements of purple and white lilacs, pots of coral 'Carefree' geraniums on lower rack of buffet and clustered at base of tree on terrace floor. Ready for family on Memorial Day!*

RIGHT: *Den in the home of a young family. Handsome copper fireplace; handmade Mexican tiles on floor; Tiffany shade; Haitian painting. Potted plant near stairs as safety reminder. Copper laundry boiler filled with* Magnolia soulangeana *branches and Virginia bluebells. At corner of stairs, wild pear blossoms. Under lamp shade, arrangement of Darwin Hybrid tulips 'Dover'.*

May Day! Restored log cabin in Wisconsin Kettle Moraine farmland. Antique candle box hung on door with apple blossoms, pansies, and tulips welcomes visitors. On the chopping block, an old wooden bowl holds early double tulips 'Peach Blossom'. On top of the antique spice cabinet is a modern blown glass vase with apple blossoms stretching far up on the log and plaster wall. A welcoming doorway!

Bougainvillea

Vines

If you have any space around your house, or near your garden, where you can plant at least two vines, do so. One might give you blossoms all summer; one could serve you all year. The usefulness of vines is legion: they furnish shade on an open porch, they hide stark poles and trash areas, they give you privacy. Some furnish fragrance as well as color. If you can't grow your own vines you'll have to haunt your friends, your florist, and/or your supermarket to get them. Here are some vines that are easy to grow outdoors and very decorative indoors:

Bougainvillea: brilliant evergreen vines growing only in frost-free areas, Zones 9 and 10, Arizona, Texas, Southern California, and Florida. Loves rich soil and needs heavy feeding to grow as a vine or even a shrubby tree up to 20 feet. Scarlet, salmon, magenta, reddish purple flowers.

Bittersweet

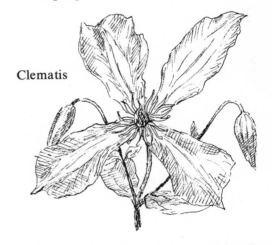

Clematis

Bittersweet *(Celastrus scandens):* probably on the "untouchable" list in your state, which means that you are not allowed to pick it in places where it grows wild. If you plant it yourself, be sure you have at least two plants near each other; it takes two to pollinate the flowers. The vines are very hardy. The berries, in late September or early October, are bright yellow. Cut the vine, take it into your house, and watch the skins pop on each berry, showing the brilliant orange shade beneath the yellow coat.

Clematis: large-flowered hybrids, flowers 4–7 inches wide. Very showy, climbing woody vine; fragile stems need to be supported on trellis fence or wire mesh. Hardy from Zone 2 southward; must have full sun, neutral soil. An "old wives' tale" says it loves bits of old plaster mixed with soil!

The best known hybrid is *C. jackmanii*, a violet purple. After that there are eight or nine beauties, among them: *J. Henryi*, very large, cameolike white flowers; 'Nelly Moser', pale mauve with reddish markings; 'Ernest Markham', deep red; 'Ramona', lavender blue. Besides these hybrids, there is a fall-blooming Japanese species, *C. paniculata*, which is a rampant grower with clusters of small fragrant white flowers that are displayed from late August to frost.

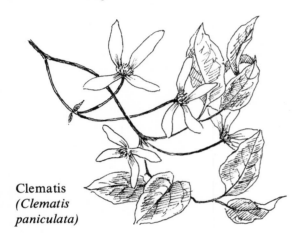

Clematis
(*Clematis paniculata*)

Confederate jasmine *(Trachelospernum jasminoides):* a high-climbing Chinese vine with evergreen foliage. Very fragrant white starlike flowers. It is widely planted in the South.

Confederate Jasmine

Smilax: vine used to decorate for special occasions in the South, for example, at Christmas or for weddings. Feathery, elegant white bloom. Easy to drape around mantels or tables.

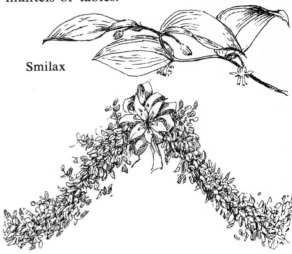

Smilax

Winter creeper *(Euonymus radicans):* an evergreen vine, very hardy, superb for covering brick or stone. Oval small leaf, finely toothed, dark, lustrous. Will grow in sun or shade. Hardy from Zone 3 south.

Winter Creeper

Besides these outdoor vines there are some vines you can grow in your home. Ask your florist what he can get for you. English ivy, no matter what variety, will grow in shade or semishade. If you have a sunny window, try little pots of jasmine and the lovely, bridal stephanotis.

Herbs

Besides being delicious additions to your gourmet recipes, herbs are so fascinating a study that whole books have been written about them: their history; their place in Bible literature; the references to them in Shakespeare's plays; their use in medicine, especially by the American Indians. Some herbs are so beautiful that they should be added to your flower border, if you are fortunate enough to have a little space to put them. You can grow some on your kitchen windowsill, then plant others outdoors in the spring when seedlings are on the market. They will give you great pleasure and will last at least two weeks in your decorating arrangements.

Lemon Balm

Lavender

Lemon Balm *(Melissa officinalis):* long-lasting, green, perennial. This was the "balm" used to crown kings. It will take over your herb bed if you let it.

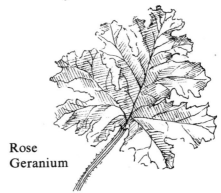

Rose Geranium

Lavender *(Lavendula spica):* lilac blue flowers with a delightful scent; perennial and ornamental.

Rose geranium *(Pelargonium graveolens):* the rose-scented group of geraniums with deeply cut foliage and lavender blooms. One, 'Attar of Roses', is the basis of perfume. 'Grey Lady Plymouth', has variegated foliage, and 'Rose' is a sweet-scented old favorite.

19

Sweet Basil

Sweet basil *(Ocimum basilicum)* 'Dark Opal': deep maroon leaf. Handsome to look at as well as to taste. Aromatic, annual.

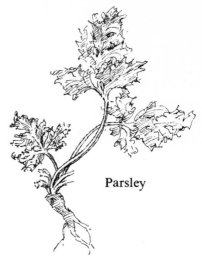

Parsley

Parsley *(Petroselinum crispum):* deep green, airy spaces in leaves, lasts long in arrangements. Biennial. Good to taste and to keep you healthy.

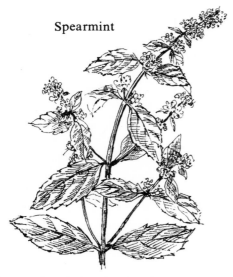

Spearmint

Spearmint *(Mentha spicata):* most used for cooking and in drinks; perennial and hardy. It, too, will take over your herb bed if you let it! Some Herb Society members recommend planting all mints and lemon balm in tin cans that can be sunk into your border and will contain the roots.

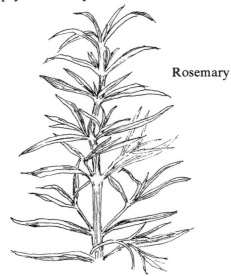

Rosemary

Rosemary *(Rosmarinus officinalis):* evergreen shrub not hardy in the North; narrow green leaves and lovely blue flowers. This is a prize possession.

You will notice that the groups of plants used in the home as potted decorations are not included here. They are so varied (small or large, with or without bloom) that they must be discussed in a different section (see pages 47–67).

20

After this brief review of the material you might choose for decorating your home, there is still one possibility to consider. If you do *not* have a green thumb and have too many other things to keep your hands busy besides growing flowers, don't forget that there are many places where you can find the material you want. First, of course, there's the florist. Some wonderful flowers and greens are available there. There are always daisies, gladioluses, carnations, roses, chrysanthemums, snapdragons, and stock. In the spring your florist can supply you with crocuses, narcissuses, and tulips, to say nothing of the heady hyacinths he'll be happy to procure for you. You can also find Dutch iris in Wedgwood blue, white, and yellow; exquisite ranunculuses in orange, pink, and yellow; deep-colored anemones of blue, red, and pink; and the newest variety of petunias. Of course, there are lilies—not just the familiar white "Easter" lily but eight to ten sorts available if you ask for them. And for extra joy of faraway places, there is the fluffy yellow acacia, available in March and April.

Calendulas, in lemon yellow or gold, will bring spring to your home in March; buy sweet peas in April if you live in the South or West. When May comes you'll find so many blooming geraniums, petunias, and pansies in supermarkets and on growers' stands, you'll have a hard time choosing. In June and July blooms are everywhere—if not in your yard (lilacs, peonies, iris, marigolds, zinnias) at least in your neighbor's or at the roadside stands. By August the chrysanthemums and asters, celosias and salvias should be available in the middle and northern states. In the Northwest the hybrid and speciosum lilies are opening. In the tropical South there should be all the summer annuals plus the patent-leather flower *(Anthurium)*, croton leaves, and bird-of-paradise *(Strelitzia)*. In the tropical West you can find the *Pyracantha* shrub, oleanders, palm fronds, and hibiscus.

In the fall there are gold and red-leaved branches of trees and shrubs at your local greenhouse, plus fascinating gourds and dried flowers—and in November bunches of bright bittersweet for your Thanksgiving table. From Oregon at Christmas comes English holly, thick with red berries. And from the Southeast, American holly, brilliant poinsettias *(Euphorbia pulcherrima)*, red or white camellias, and the airy, decorative smilax vine to decorate your home with elegance.

All you have to do is to become familiar with the vast variety of living materials available that will add beauty to your home, then pick or buy a few flowers or greens to suit your taste. After you have them at home, there are a few simple steps that will help you keep your flowers and greens fresh and beautiful. That's what you're going to learn about now.

Conditioning
Cut Plants and Flowers

CONDITIONING is a term used to describe various methods of preserving the color, strength, and life of fresh flowers, greens, or shrubs after they have been cut.

Some experts suggest that you put a tablet of aspirin in daisies . . . a teaspoon of sugar in roses . . . even a copper penny in chrysanthemums or tulips to keep them healthy. Others consider these hints "folklore" and ignore them. The best thing to do is to read everything you can about keeping flowers and plants fresh, try some of the suggestions, and decide for yourself which methods work best.

IMPORTANCE OF CONDITIONING
There are two outstanding reasons for conditioning plants, one practical and the other aesthetic. Living plants are costly even if you grow them yourself. If you buy flowers at the florist or the supermarket you know that even ordinary spring tulips, snapdragons, or summer-flowering mock-orange branches are not always cheap. But the pleasure these flowers afford is worth the cost if you can be sure that they will last five days or more in their arrangements.

You must also consider your time. If you devote any part of your busy day to the art of flower arranging, the result must certainly be worthy of your effort.

Both your money and your time will be well spent if the arrangements look fresh and beautiful and remain that way for as long as possible. Conditioning helps to assure that they will.

VITAL REQUIREMENTS FOR CONDITIONING

There are three vital and very simple requirements for conditioning any living flower, shrub, or green. The first is *water—water—water*. It can stand repeating because water is absolutely essential to every living plant. Here is another area where you have to make your own decision between cold and hot water for conditioning. The firm rule of using cold (or cool) water has been challenged recently by those who prefer using hot water and letting it cool while the flowers or shrubs are being conditioned. Many people prefer the "cold (or cool) water" method. You should try both methods and see which works best for you.

The second requirement is to control the *temperature* of the area where the flowers or shrubs are left to soak up their water. If you condition flowers on top of a radiator or near a burning fireplace, you will not get anything but tired, hot plants. They thrive at a temperature of about 40 degrees, so the conditioning will be most effective in the coolest part of the house or apartment. Your refrigerator is perfect for this provided, of course, you can find room in it!

The third requirement is to place the flowers and greens you are conditioning in a location that has *shaded light and no drafts.* Sometimes a room with air conditioning makes a good spot for fussy flowers to spend a day and night. Nobody expects you to darken the whole house for hours while your greens and flowers soak up water. On the other hand, if you have only a little space in the kitchen or family-room area to put your flowers, try to find a place where the bright sunshine won't beat down on them.

STEPS IN CONDITIONING

"Fresh-picked" flowers. If you pick your own flowers and shrubs, carry water with you. Lightweight plastic pails can be purchased in hardware stores. Some types have a divider that will help you sort your flowers or greens as you cut them. Put just a few inches of water in each side so that the pail will not be heavy. The only other accessories you will need are a flower clipper, a sharp flower knife, a candle stub, and a small box of matches.

Cut the stems on a slant (don't pull them); pull off the lower leaves and put them in water immediately.

Removing the lower foliage of plants before you put them in to condition is a general rule that applies to all cut plants, shrubs, and vines, as well as to flowers. Stems and foliage below the waterline become soft and slimy in a short time. Actually, they are decaying, and as they decay they form bacteria that will dirty the water and destroy the cut plants in a day or two. Flowers and shrubs will last twice as long if the water they are put in remains clean. This is why the lower leaves must be taken off, not only before you put the plants into water to condition, but also when you arrange them in their permanent container. It is also a good idea to clean any dusty leaves and flowers with a sponge or cloth.

If you have an arrangement in mind before you pick your flowers, you can save time by sorting the blossoms as you put them into the two-sided pail: reds, pinks, and whites in one compartment; yellows, scarlets, and blues in another. Then take them into the house to finish the conditioning. Clip or crush the stem of each bloom, take off more bottom foliage, if necessary, then put the flowers into a deep container of cool, clean water for an hour or two to soak up all the liquid they can hold.

"Store-bought" flowers. If you buy your flowers or shrubs from a florist, they will probably arrive with the stems freshly cut and the bottom leaves taken off. Flowers that you buy at a supermarket have probably been sitting in the same water all day, getting warmer and more tired by the hour. To recapture their original color and vigor, take them home as fast as possible and give them the same care you would give your home-grown flowers. Cut the stems firmly on a slant, strip off the leaves at the bottom of the stems, and put the flowers into deep, cool water for at least an hour or, if you can, for a whole day and night.

CONDITIONING SPECIFIC GROUPS OF FLOWERS

Flowers can be divided into groups according to their conditioning needs. All you have to do is look at the stem, and you will know what to do to help the flower draw in as much water as it can hold.

Flowers with thin stems. Some of the most popular in this category are:

Narcissuses, tulips, and ageratums; all springtime beauties.

English daisies, carnations, and petunias; available at the florist.

Zinnias, marigolds, and geraniums; summertime bloomers; in tropical Zones 9 and 10 year round.

All these flowers respond to the same treatment. Cut ½ inch off the bottom of each stem. Then plunge them into cool fresh water for as long a time as you can give them. Two hours will make a tremendous difference in their lives, but they must have at least an hour. Keep them in a cool room if the refrigerator is full of other essentials.

They all need a large, deep container so that they are not crowded. Remove the foliage, but don't throw it away. If your narcissuses have lovely, tall, slender leaves you are lucky. They are often sold without leaves. Put all these leaves into a separate bowl or beaker of water and let them wait in the refrigerator or in a cool place until you can arrange the flowers. Then use them to accent your arrangement.

Flowers with thick stems. The second class of flowers are those with thick, hard, or woody stems. You may have some of them growing in your garden; if not, you can find them at the florist or at roadside stands in spring and summer. These tall, large-bloomed flowers have to be treated carefully to be sure they absorb enough water. Crush the ends of their big stems so that plenty of water can get through. This can be done with either a knife or a scissors. Or you can buy a special little rubber-headed hammer at a florist's or gardening shop to crush the stems.

Here are some thick-stemmed flowers you may want to use:

Iris: Cut or buy a stalk with the lower blossoms just ready to open. Condition the foliage in a separate vase. If you take off all used-up blooms as they fade and dry, you will have a beautiful stalk for at least a week.

Peonies: These lovely flowers can be cut (or bought) in bud or full bloom. Take off the leaves and condition them separately in the refrigerator; add them to your arrangement later. Just two stalks will fill your home with fragrance. If the flower-head droops, use #24 florist's wire to strengthen the stem. Hold the stem and wire together in your left hand, then turn the top of the wire into an angle fitting around the stem next to the blossom. Turn the stem around and around in your left hand while you twist the wire around the stem as far as you need

it. Don't let it catch on the foliage. The wire will not show when you place the flower into your arrangement..

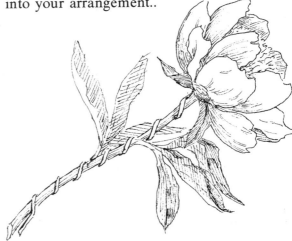

Chrysanthemums: There are all kinds and varieties of this marvelous flower from small daisylike forms to little button shapes to huge "football" heads. Always cut when blossom is completely open. Then, crush the stem with hammer or clipper before putting it in water. Never pull a petal off a chrysanthemum. If one is blemished, pinch it off. If it leaves a hole in a big blossom, drop a bit of candle wax, the same color, over the hole to hold the blossom together.

Delphiniums: This perennial flower can almost be considered the queen of the summer garden. It is so difficult to find these fresh spikes at a florist that it is worth the trouble to plant two or three clumps in your garden, if you can. If you grow the plants, cut the stalk before the lowest blossoms are completely open. Take off the lower leaves and remove the long side stems that detract from the main blossom. Then cut the stem again, on a slant, and put it into deep water for at least three hours. If you want to keep the blossoms from opening until you make your arrangement, put them in the bedroom where you can draw the curtains all day and keep the flowers cool. Once conditioned, delphiniums will last for six or seven days.

25

Stock: These marvelous scented flowers usually grow best in the florist's greenhouse or in Zones 6, 7, 8, where there is little danger of frost. If you grow stock in your garden, cut it when the blossom is three-quarters to fully open. Stock has very soft leaves which disintegrate quickly if left under water. On the other hand, its stems are so hard that the ends must be mashed with a hammer to allow the water to be absorbed.

Snapdragons: These spiky flowers are one of the "backbones" of flower gardens and flower arrangements. They grow equally well in cold and subtropical zones. The new E-1 hybrids have been given so much attention by plant breeders that not only are they almost completely disease-resistant but the very shape of the blossom of some varieties has been changed from a "snap" to an open, azalealike bloom. If you grow them, cut the flowers when three-fourths to fully open.

Snapdragons respond dramatically to having their stems cut under water. If they look droopy, fill a big pitcher with cool water, hold each stem under the surface of the water, and cut off ½ inch. In ten minutes they will take on new life. You can almost hear them rustle!

Gladioluses: These are flowers from greenhouse or tropical zone or above the Mason-Dixon line. If you grow them in your garden, take them inside when the lower buds are just beginning to show color. Many growers recommend that you break the stems instead of cutting them. After you have arranged them, be sure to take the dead blossoms off and shorten the stems every few days as the upper blossoms open. They will look lovely even when they are only a few inches high, tucked into a little bowl on your coffee table.

Flowers with hollow stems. A third group of flowers, such as dahlias and African daisies, have hollow stems. Dahlia stems are wide as well as hollow, and need to be sealed to keep the important juice in the stalk. To do this, place the stems in scalding hot water for about a minute. Always put paper over the saucepan and stick the stem of the flower through that into the water. This will keep the steam away from the flowers. If African daisies begin to wilt after they are cut, you can revive them by putting the stems in hot water following the instructions above.

Flowers with stems that "bleed" when cut. The only other group of flowers that need special conditioning is the kind with stems that emit a sticky, milky liquid. The stalk and the blossoms cannot survive without this lifegiving liquid, so it must be sealed in as soon as the stem is cut. This is why you take an old candle stump and matches with you when you go into your garden to cut daylilies. Light the candle and sear the bottom of the stalk with the flame before you put the flower into the pail of water. Although the stem is closed at the bottom, the water will still enter through the outside of the stem. When you buy these flowers from the florist, you will find the ends of the stems already blackened. Keep the flowers in deep water for at least an hour once you have them in your house.

Three other flowers that you may enjoy using also emit this milky liquid. In each case, the end of the stem must be seared as soon as it is cut, then placed in deep water. One is the Oriental poppy *(Papaver orientale)*, a lovely flower that blooms in early summer, then seemingly dries up and disappears until the end of August when it starts its fall growth. If you grow this flower, cut it when the petals are ready to unfold, not in tight buds. Another is the balloon flower *(Platycodon grandiflorum)*, one of the most de-

pendable perennials you can grow. It is usually a heavenly shade of blue, and it blooms all summer. The third is the poinsettia *(Euphorbia pulcherrima)*, which grows in Arizona, California, or other areas in Zones 9 and 10.

Don't forget that whenever you take these flowers out to change the water and cut the stems, you have to sear the ends again.

CONDITIONING SMALL FLOWERS

When you pick or buy pansies, sweet peas, violets, or nasturtiums, cut ½ inch off the bottom of the stems, and tie about ten flowers together in a compact bunch with soft green florist's twine or soft green florist's tape. Then put the bunches in water. You can probably find a place for these small flowers in your refrigerator for an hour or two. When they have regained their freshness, tuck the bunches into an arrangement or display them alone.

SPECIAL TREATMENT FOR SPECIAL FLOWERS

Roses. Roses should be cut, either by you or your florist, when they are still in bud but almost ready to unfold. Cut or buy them with as much stem as you need. You can always cut some off later. Always cut or pinch off the thorns on the stem. Work quickly to take off all the lower leaves and cut the ends of the stems with a knife. Do not use a cutter; it squeezes the stem too much. Be sure the stem is cut at enough of a slant to take in all the water it can hold. Put cotton, lightly soaked in water, around the base of each stem and tie waxed paper around it. Roll the rosebud carefully in waxed paper so it will not open. Then lay the roses in the refrigerator all that day and night. Take the roses out next morning, cut the stems again, and arrange them as you planned. As soon as the heat of the room reaches them, the roses will open and bloom just as you want them to do. And they will last perfectly for almost a week.

favorite method, but first you might like to try this: Cut the lilacs late in the afternoon. Take off all the leaves and little stems. Make a crosswise cut across the bottom of the stem and pull the skin off the branch about 2 or 3 inches above the cut end. Then put the whole bunch of blossoms into a washtub full of cool water. Let it stay overnight. When you take it out the next morning the flowers will be ready to arrange and will stay fresh for days.

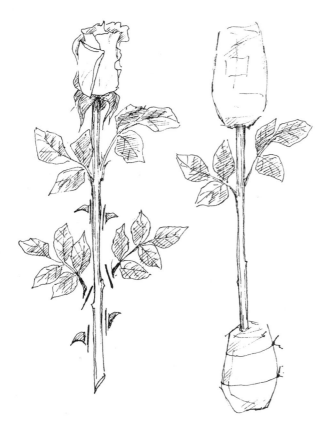

Lilacs *(Syringa)*. There are many ways to keep lilacs fresh and vital. Flowers, like cakes and soufflés, respond differently to different people. You will probably find your own

Lilies *(Lilium)*. Lilies are among the most beautiful flowers in the world, particularly in the last twenty years when the hybrids and species have been bred to a new distinction. Only recently have florists realized the possibilities of carrying these flowers for their customers. And gardeners all over the country have ordered the wonderful bulbs to plant in their own gardens.

A stalk of lily, cut and conditioned, will last at least two weeks and bring pleasure to everyone who sees it. If you grow lilies, be careful to cut only half of the foliage with your flowers. The remaining leaves are needed to nourish the bulb for next year. Whether you grow lilies or buy them at the florist, be sure you get a stalk with at least two flowers that are open. After you have cut the stem, split it and place it in deep, cool water overnight. Next day you can arrange it. The other buds will open day by day. If there is danger of the gold pollen on the stamen staining the lily itself—or anything underneath it—put your hand inside the blossom and pinch off the stamen.

One of the most reliable varieties is 'Enchantment', an upright-flowering Asiatic hybrid that blooms in June. If you like the trumpet-shaped lily, there's the Olympic hybrid, in mid-July—sometimes white, sometimes pink, sometimes green. And just in time for Labor Day, with no labor, come the wonderful *Lilium speciosum,* some in white, some in red, and looking for all the world like something from *Alice in Wonderland.* One slim stalk will rise up from your living-room table with a graceful spirit—and you will feel new spirit yourself, just from looking at it. Try it!

CONDITIONING SHRUBS

Shrubs as well as flowers need conditioning. The great difference between the two is that the stems of shrubs are so hard and tough that they need to be cut crosswise in order to absorb the water they need. In addition to removing the lower foliage, pull back the bark on the bottom of the stem about 2 or 3 inches to hasten the absorption of water. Put the shrub branches in deep, cool water in a cool room for as long as you possibly can before arranging them. All varieties of shrubs respond well to this treatment.

Flowering shrubs. There are almost as many flowering shrubs as there are flowers for you to choose for your home. Remember that the flowering shrubs that are fragrant will double the pleasure you derive from any arrangement.

Evergreens. Evergreen branches are as sturdy as they are beautiful. Sometimes they need to be cleaned, under running water with a brush or sponge, before they are put to condition in cool water. Since their stems are tough, they may need two or three cuts to make sure the water can be absorbed. Once they are full of water they will last weeks, sometimes months, in an arrangement.

Green shrubs. Green shrubs provide branches to feature by themselves or be used as fillers with flowers. Like all living plants, they must be trimmed, the bases of the stems split open, and then put into deep water to soak up as much moisture as they can. They are not inexpensive, but if conditioned properly, they will last several weeks. You can preserve some of these shrubs in glycerine so they will last forever. (See pages 82–94.)

CONDITIONING VINES

Treat most vines as you would any flower. Make sure the leaves are clean, take off foliage near the cut ends, crush the ends a little, and put the vines in clear, cool water for at least an hour before you arrange them.

English ivy should be put completely underwater for a half hour. It will root in the water you arrange it in and grow where you put it in your home.

Clematis could be considered an alcoholic. A tablespoon of alcohol in the conditioning water will make it last much longer and look more beautiful.

Bittersweet should be started in water, to soften the stem, so you can bend it in the shape you desire. But once the water is gone, the vine will last all winter with no water at all.

CONDITIONING HERBS

Condition herbs as you would any other greens: Place them in cool water, with the stems cut, and add fresh water daily. They would benefit tremendously by an hour in the refrigerator, too.

CONDITIONING LEAVES

The leaves of many flowers are so beautiful in themselves that you can use them without any blossoms at all, if you prefer. Or, you can use them with their own flowers or with completely unrelated flowers. Here are some that have especially beautiful leaves.

Narcissuses: wonderful clumps of tall, slender foliage.

Tulips: gray-green or dark green, laced with red lines in the new *Gregii* hybrids.

Iris: sharp, sword-shaped, tall.

Delphiniums: large leaves of elegant form, divided, long-stemmed. Keep well when taken off stalk and conditioned separately.

Geraniums: many colors and varieties with differing design. Some are round and green, some show oval marks; some are divided, some have color; many are sweet-scented, some are spice-scented. All leaves are decorative; will last at least a week after being conditioned.

Peonies: indispensable, both in shape and quality. The color in summer is a deep, fresh green. The shape is in three parts, each sculptured in three, five, or six graceful patterns.

Wild ginger: wonderful heart-shaped leaf, ground cover.

Crotons: grown for their leaves, which can be flat or narrow and twisted. From white with green "veins" and edging to gorgeous striped or patterned leaves of pink, brown, yellow, red.

Leaves require the same vital steps in conditioning as flowers do. Take the leaves off the flowers. Cut the stems, put them in a separate jar, and find a space for them in that overloaded refrigerator for an hour or even overnight. You will marvel at the richness the peony leaf will give to a big mass of blooms or even a single blossom. In September and October these leaves develop wine-red and orange shades in the green, making them perfect for Thanksgiving bouquets and arrangements.

Learning to condition your cut plants is a simple matter. But do not underestimate it. It is the most important step in achieving the joy of decorating your home with fresh flowers and greens.

ABC's of Flower Arranging

Every craft and art form requires some special equipment. What special tools will you need to make flower arrangements that are beautiful enough to decorate your home? Not very many.

First, you have to have cutting tools. If you go into your garden to pick flowers or greens or shrubs, you probably own a flower cutter and sharp pruning shears. If you don't, these are not hard to find. However, the most satisfactory tool for cutting stems is a pair of Japanese flower scissors. Only about 6 inches long, they have curved, wide "handles" and 2-inch sharp blades with pointed ends. Look for them in garden supply shops or Japanese shops, or ask your florist where you can find a pair. There are companion scissors that are longer (about 8 inches), narrower, and lighter in weight. These are excellent to trim delicate greens, blossoms, and completed arrangements, and are well worth any trouble you have searching for them. These two pairs of scissors will last for many years and bring you great satisfaction.

If you have shrubs growing in your garden you will need tough pruning shears. Indoors you might prefer lighter-weight shears for splitting woody branches or thick-stemmed flowers. There's one that is 8 inches long, has a spring between the handles, and is very handy.

There are some flowers that it is wise to cut with a knife instead of shears. The Japanese don't have a special corner on the knife

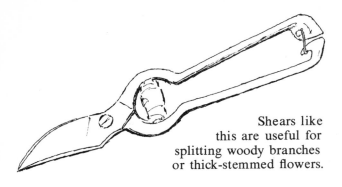

Shears like this are useful for splitting woody branches or thick-stemmed flowers.

Any sharp stainless steel knife can be used to cut stems that would be squeezed by scizzors.

market. Any American or German stainless-steel knife is excellent. If you can find a Henekel knife bearing the little Twins trade-mark on it, you will find it worth its price. When you have found the perfect gardening knife, announce to your family that it is *only* for flowers, not for paring carrots or whit-

tling! It's smart to commandeer a special drawer near the kitchen sink, one that only you and special, "licensed" flower arrangers may use!

What else do you need to keep in that special drawer? Not the containers—the vases or bowls or baskets or platters in which to arrange your flowers or branches. There are so many of these that you will need a special shelf (or shelves) for them. But in your drawer you can keep all the wonderful helpers that will make flower arranging easier and more effective. Here are some of them:

Metal needle holders. To hold flowers, leaves, branches in the container. Stainless steel, they won't rust. They're heavy, inexpensive, come in round, oval, or rectangular shape and in plain steel, copper, black, or green. Two sizes oval and two sizes round will probably meet your needs for most arrangements.

Metal pin cups and needle holders—available in many shapes, sizes, and colors.

Metal pin cups. To hold water as well as the arrangement. They come in stainless steel, in different shapes and sizes, and in black or green.

You might like to treat yourself to a decorative brass pin cup, about 4 inches across and 1½ inches deep, to use for special arrangements on a black or natural-wood tray.

Metal frogs. Strong, waffle-topped holders to use for heavy or long-stemmed flowers or greens.

Rolls of fine chicken wire. Use the kind with 1-inch holes to bunch into shapes that fit into tall containers. It will hold stemmed shrubs or greens or heavy flowers in place.

Posey Klay. Specially prepared clay that will keep a needle holder, frog, or pin cup in place. Roll a small amount of Posey Klay between your hands to warm it up, then fit it underneath the dry edge of the flower holder

Some flower holders are decorative as well as functional.

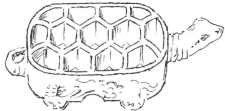

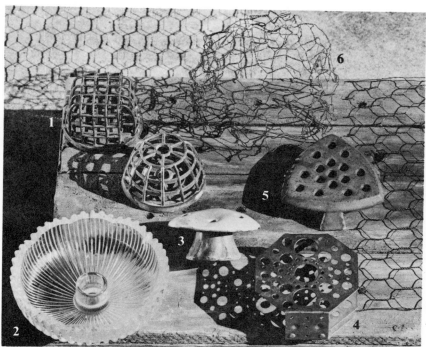

1. Strong, waffle-topped "frogs" to hold large flowers or branches.
2. Crystal container, which fits over a candle, in a candleholder. Ozite is fiitted around candle to hold flowers or greens.
3. Handmade ceramic "toadstool" to hold flowers.
4. Stainless-steel modern "frog" to hold long-stemmed branches or flowers.
5. Handmade ceramic "frog" to hold flowers.
6. Chicken wire crushed to fit into a large-mouthed container. Background and at right, uncrushed wire.

and press it into the container. It will not stain silver or glass, wood or plastic. It's the most delightful invention since the electric light!

Keep a box in the drawer to hold the cutting tools, another to hold the pin holders and the Posey Klay, and you will still have more than half the drawer left for the other "mechanics"!

Let's see what other helpers might be needed.

Floral tape. One small roll of brown; one roll of green. This narrow, useful tape is self-sticking on one side. Use it to lengthen stems of flowers too short to reach water in your arrangement. Slip the short stem into a longer stem of another flower and seal the two together with the green tape. The short stem will still receive water through the long stem to keep it fresh. The brown tape will be invisible to stake shrubs or dried flowers.

The green tape can be used to stake green flowers and plants.

Long green florist's wires. Use #18 for strengthening stiff flowers like chrysanthemums, gladioluses, dahlias; #24 is for roses, tulips, carnations. Twist the wire loosely around the stem of the flower. It will hold the flower head up and, since it's pliable, you can bend the stem into any position.

Spool of florist's green wire. Use to wire evergreens, cones, anything!

Spool of green corsage twine. Use to tie bunches of tender-stemmed flowers.

Twist'ems. Indispensable lengths of thin wire enclosed in green paper. You can use them for 1001 purposes, from attaching stakes to flowers and shrubs to holding nuts and cones onto Christmas wreaths.

1. Rolls of brown and green floral tape, self-sticking on one side.
2. Japanese flower scissors.
3. Posey Klay, to keep everything securely in its place.
4. Spool of florist's green wire.
5. Twist'ems, short and long. Thin wire enclosed in green paper.
6. Florist's green wires: #18 for strengthening stiff flowers (mums, gladioluses, dahlias); #24 for thinner flowers (roses, tulips, carnations).
7. Old Japanese mister.

1. Sprinkling can.
2. Pebbles. Several needed to hide base of pin holder.
3. Fungus pulled from an old tree. To decorate arrangement.
4. Hand-carved teakwood base to hold container of arrangement.
5. Dry, light green ozite. To be fitted into container, then soaked with water to hold flowers.

Small box of pebbles. Use to hide the pin holder in a finished arrangement.

Floral picks. These are short, pointed green wooden sticks with a thin wire fastened to the blunt end. They can be used to wire stems of apples, pears, bunches of grapes, even decorative leaves. These can be secured into an arrangement invisibly.

A block of light green ozite. You can use this in your container instead of a needle holder. It can be cut to fit any size bowl or vase or basket. It can even be fastened on top of a stainless-steel needle holder in the container. Cover the ozite with a piece of 1-inch metal chicken wire to keep it securely fastened. Once it fits in the container, add water and allow the ozite to soak it up completely. When saturated, it will hold any flower or shrub you push into it.

One advantage of using the ozite is that you can angle the flowers or greens to the side and low down in the front more easily than you can with a needle holder. You will soon learn which arrangements are best in ozite and which in needle holders. Some expert flower designers say you must leave the ozite wet and in its container even when the original arrangement is removed. A plastic bag over the container will keep the ozite moist. But if you prefer, you may remove the ozite when you remove the flowers and moisten it when you want to use it again.

A long-spouted watering can. Find a medium-size one, of copper or brass, that is not too heavy to carry to your arrangements wherever they are. If you add fresh water each day, the flowers, shrubs, or greens will last longer and look better.

With these helpers at hand, you will find that arranging flowers can really be a "breeze"!

35

Tips on Arranging

After you select the flowers, or combination of flowers and greens, you want, how do you arrange them so that they look their best? You give them a design. Nelson Coon, writing in the monthly publication of the American Horticultural Society, has this to say: "Gardens can satisfy our five senses. . . . That of sight receives gratification from the beauty of basic design, including color, texture, form." This is as true of the design of a flower arrangement as it is in a garden.

If yours is a modern house and your taste leans toward modern furniture and fabrics, you will want modern arrangements in your home. The Japanese use abstract designs, so why shouldn't you? The only thing is, the Japanese must pass the most rigorous course of study and receive a diploma in a traditional school of flower arranging before they even begin to experiment. Then they either follow the rules or know what rules they are breaking. This is the difference between a Picasso painting and a three-year-old's crayon sketch. One of them has gone through the classical technique of drawing, composition, and design before he knew enough to discard the rules.

If you want to be comfortable with flowers in your home, you must study at least enough to know what you might create, even if you don't want to follow the rules all the time. So here are some fundamentals you would learn if you enrolled in a flower-arranging class. They may sound complex, but they really aren't. And there are "quickie" ways to get satisfying effects by remembering just one or two things.

First, you must remember that every flower arrangement is an individual, creative work of art. You, as the artist, can be guided by certain elements and principles of design in making the arrangement.

THE ELEMENTS OF DESIGN

Six design elements are used and combined to form your arrangement: *Space, line, form, pattern, texture,* and *color.*

Space. You must plan your arrangement so that it fits the space you've selected for it—either the concrete dimensions of the table in your entrance hall, or the imaginary limits of the space of your living room wall which will serve as a background for an important mass of summery flowers, or the windowsill in the family room where you want to place an informal arrangement. Once you have decided on the space that will frame your arrangement you will know whether the arrangement has to be taller than it is wide, wider than it is tall, what container would be suitable, and what color or kind of flower would be appropriate.

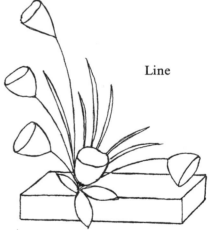

Line

Line. Line is the next element to consider. Line determines the shape, the pattern, and the movement of your arrangement. In your mind's eye you plan the line you want: vertical, diagonal, horizontal. You decide whether it should be long, short, weak, strong, or a combination of several. The line you want is the foundation of the design of your arrangement. Linear material—tall flowers, straight greens, curved lines—shapes, colors in repetition, all these create movement in the line of your design.

Form. The form of your arrangement appears when you fill in the line with flowers and greens. You can decide whether you want a massed arrangement, with the flowers put together in a solid, compact form, with few openings or "voids"; or whether you want an open kind of arrangement with flowers and greens spreading and extending, with space or "voids" an important part of the arrangement. The form can be patterned after a mathematical figure—a triangle, square, or circle—or it can be a pyramid, cube, or sphere. It can also be a freestanding form designed to be pleasing in all directions. But always remember that the form must have depth. It is not just flat.

Pattern. An element that will help you achieve depth in your arrangement is pattern. The repetition of open spaces in the arrangement will form a pattern; repetition of flowers, colors, and greens will also form a pattern.

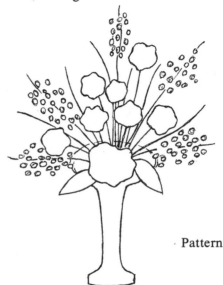

Pattern

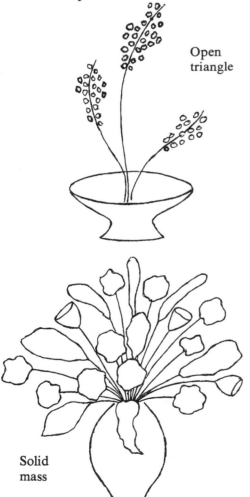

Open triangle

Solid mass

Texture. Another element that is important and will give distinction to an arrangement is its texture. Texture is the coarseness or fineness of the material. The touch or visual quality. All flowers and greens differ in the texture of their leaves or blossoms. Your taste will come to your aid at this point. You certainly would not want to combine fine lilies with rough zinnias or to select marigolds as companions to 'Peace' roses for a dinner-party arrangement. Each of these flowers is handsome in its own right and with flowers of its own kind. Variety of texture lends interest to any arrangement, but there must be some relation between the textures of the flowers you put together. Trumpet-shaped lilies would make an elegant arrangement with the tall spikes of the delphinium. The texture of zinnias, with their round, deep-colored blooms, and marigolds relate to the texture of nicotiana, snapdragon, coxcomb, or tall cosmos. 'Peace' roses would shine with stock, delicate clusters of columbine *(Aquilegia)* and ageratum, or with trailing petunias and spiked blue salvia.

Texture influences the appearance of weight and color. When you choose flowers with rough, dull texture, they should go at the bottom of the arrangement, for they seem heavy. Smooth, fine texture makes flowers seem lighter; rough texture makes them seem duller. There should also be some relation between the textures of flowers and containers, and between containers and the room or location where the arrangement is placed. For example, an antique wooden bowl filled with apple blossoms is charming in a country kitchen but would not be effective in a city living room. Nor would a heavy pottery mug be as appropriate for roses as a clear glass or porcelain vase.

Color. The last element of design is color. We think of this as an element that should not present any problem, but if we don't understand the fundamentals of color, our arrangements will not be attractive.

Let's review these fundamentals. There are three primary colors: red, blue, and yellow. They are called primary because all the other colors can be made from them.

Secondary colors are made by mixing equal amounts of the primary colors. Red and yellow make orange; blue and yellow make green; red and blue make violet. You probably are familiar with a color wheel that shows the primary colors and the secondary colors they can form. You will see that colors opposite each other on the wheel are the most stimulating: red with green, blue with orange, yellow with violet. These complementary or contrasting colors are extremely attractive in flower arrangements.

That's why you like to arrange yellow tulips and lavender lilacs together. Why pale green walls are livened by pink and red roses. Your instinct to arrange orange marigolds

with blue ageratums in midsummer comes from realizing that these two colors are especially effective together.

The complementary or contrasting colors will be more pleasing in flower arrangements if the more intense color is used in small quantities or concentrated at the base of the arrangement.

No color has to be used in its deepest value. Its lightness or darkness depends on the presence of white or black or gray in it. For instance, white added to red makes pink; white added to purple makes lavender. These are called *tints.* If you add black to red, it becomes maroon. Black to orange becomes brown. These are called *shades.* Rose is red with gray added; add gray to yellow and it becomes beige.

Knowing the colors from which these tints and shades originate helps you choose flowers or leaves that go together. If you use one color with many tints and shades of that color, you will have an arrangement that is *monochromatic.* It can give a beautiful effect. Sometimes it's modern: dark brown magnolia leaves and lemon yellow Fuji chrysanthemum blossoms. Sometimes it's primitive: different tints or shades of red zinnias—rose, pink, coral—in a wooden bowl. This kind of flower arrangement is often used in a modern city room that is decorated in one color. It can also be used to complement the color of a wall or the upholstery of a couch or chair.

Red, orange, and yellow are warm colors. They are visually stimulating and look best when used in relatively small areas. Green, blue, and violet are cool colors. They are good support or background colors and look well in relatively large areas. An area that is light in color appears larger than one that is dark. Deeper colors look better if they seem to support lighter colors. These few basic facts about color will help you in arranging flowers effectively.

THE PRINCIPLES OF DESIGN

The principles of design are more abstract than the elements about which you have just been reading. They lend special distinction to your work. In order to make a really attractive flower arrangement, five principles must be considered: *balance, dominance, contrast, rhythm, proportion and scale.*

Balance. Let's translate our six principles into a bowl of pink snapdragons and flaming orange marigolds and start with the principle of balance. If you place the spike of the tallest snapdragon firmly in the center of a pin holder in a round bowl and begin to add the other snapdragons, interlaced with the marigolds, until you come to the fullest blossoms cut short at the bottom, you're getting balance in a symmetrical arrangement. But if you've placed your pin holder over to the left of either a round or a square or oval bowl, with the tallest snapdragon slanting beyond the rim, you'll have to save lots of the shorter stalks of snapdragons to balance the arrangement with added weight on the other side. And three fat marigolds in varying short heights placed where the two sides come together will make it possible for you to enjoy your efforts without the fear that the whole will lack visual balance.

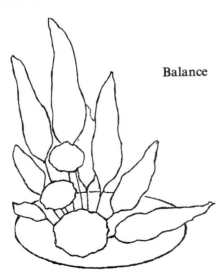

Balance

The central position of the marigolds helps the balance of your arrangement. You never want to make this center too obvious. You can lead the eye to the center with smaller, taller marigolds, so they will not stand out too obviously. But there should be a larger or darker color flower or some greenery near the base of your arrangement.

Dominance. In the bowl of snapdragons and marigolds, decide which color you want to dominate. Don't choose four of each or ten of each. Have five pink flowers and three orange; or the other way around. In addition to having one color dominate in the arrangement, you can emphasize one texture of foliage over another, one form of flower, one size of blossom dominating the rest. Use two or three times as much of one thing as you do of another. All this lends interest and variety.

Contrast. Another method of obtaining variety in any design is by contrast. Your selection of the silky, spiky snapdragons and the crêpe-papery spheres of marigolds achieves a contrast of flower shapes. The marvelous combination of unusual colors provides another. All parts of the design that emphasize differences give special distinction to your arrangement: the heights of the snapdragons—no stems just the same length—the size of the marigolds—the "voids" being different in shape and size. Even the lines of the arrangement, some vertical, some horizontal, some curving, all provide the contrast that lifts your design from the banal to the artistic.

Rhythm. Rhythm is not easily defined in design. We can hear it in music, recognize it in nature, and if it's present in flower design, we feel it. The position of the flowers and greens, their size and color, create a feeling of smoothness that leads our eye, our imagination through the whole arrangement and gives us pleasure. In our imaginary

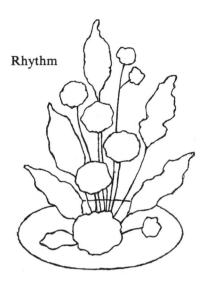

Rhythm

tion of the size and number of flowers to their container and the relation of the size and shape of the container to the area in which it is placed. You aren't going to put one football chrysanthemum into a little bud vase or place a bud vase against a big wall that needs a spreading mass. *Scale* (how big?) is the size relationship of each component part of an arrangement. You aren't going to combine trumpet lilies with little purple pansies unless they are part of a tremendous arrangement of lilies, delphiniums, roses, and cyclamens and you use the pansies, in fat bunches, tucked into the edge of your container.

These are the basics of flower arranging. If they don't all seem to be clear to you as you read them for the first time, don't worry. After you begin to work with your arrangements, you will understand them and find yourself putting them into practice. Here are some "quickies" that you might find useful. Can you see which of the elements and principles they represent?

1. Let your tallest flowers rise at least two and one-half times the height of your con-

arrangement of snapdragons and marigolds, let's try an easy exercise. Find a long marigold branch ending in a bud and place it in the midst of the tallest snapdragons. Then place two or four more, each shorter and larger in blossom than the last, almost, but not quite, in a line from the top to the lowest point for which you've saved the most enormous. Now you've created rhythm through both color and form. (An expert flower-arranger friend vows she can win the approval of almost any garden club by this "neatest trick of the week"—repeating like flowers graduating in size from top to bottom.)

Repetition can also be used to give the effect of gradual change: in weight, from light to heavy; in texture, from fine to course; in color, from light to dark, bright to dull, value to value. Rhythm can come from repeating in different tints instead of the same color; or by using two or three small round flowers in place of one large one. All the elements of design can be used to give rhythm to your arrangement, particularly the lines you choose.

Proportion and Scale. For the last two principles, just use good sense and your own taste. *Proportion* (how many?) is the rela-

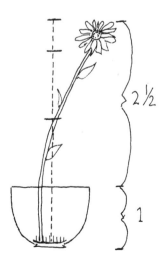

40

tainer or one and one-half times its width.

2. Give the top flower in a symetrical or a line arrangement twice as much space between it and the second tallest as there will be between the second and all the others that follow it down.

3. Use little buds and small flowers at the height of the arrangement, larger and heavier ones as you go down.

4. Use white or paler blooms high up, or outlining the perimeter; use heavier, darker shades lower down, often forming a focal point at the base.

5. Let individual flowers seem to come from the center of your arrangement.

6. Turn some of your flowers in profile; don't let them all face you.

7. Tuck one or two blossoms, in a mass arrangement, behind others. It will make your arrangement leap into a third dimension like a stereoptican.

8. "Break" the rim of your arrangement by letting the deepest, largest flower or lowest leaf or green hang out over the edge—or open up a huge Darwin Hybrid tulip's three lower petals so the stunning base draws the eye beyond the rim.

9. Solve the problem of small or weak-stemmed flowers such as sweet peas, pansies, lily-of-the-valley, nasturtiums, violets by bunching them together and tying them with green florist's twine or twisting green floral tape around the stems, then tucking them in as a single unit. You can do this with larger flowers too, such as spray carnations or even pompon chrysanthemums, so that you can place them in graduated position, some taller than others. You can then be sure they will stay that way, once they're in the arrangement. If the water is high enough to cover the stems, but the vase too deep for them to reach the pin holder, you can tape the bunch onto a long florist's pick or the stem of a strong flower that you've discarded.

10. *Don't let your mechanics show.* In a shallow container, cover the base of the pin holder with a lovely leaf, or with extra greens or pebbles.

The Japanese art of arranging flowers and greens is a subject in itself, but you can begin by remembering the three symbols of *Heaven, Man,* and *Earth* in connection with the varying lengths of flowers or branches: two and one-half times the depth of the container or one and one-half times its diameter for the *Heaven* height; the second line, *Man,* is two-thirds the length of the first; and the third line, *Earth,* is one-third the length of the first. It is customary to use three or five or even seven flowers or greens in the arrangement. The Japanese call this art of flower arranging *Ikebana.* Another useful style for modern decorating is called *Moribana,* or "water-viewing," which allows the use of more greens or flowers. But all Japanese arrangements must be triangular in shape and seem always to come from the center of the pin holder, as if they were naturally growing there. There are many books on the subject. Study illustrations of the authentic Japanese arrangements and then try your hand at it. For arrangements "in the Japanese manner," you can use low pottery bowls, rectangular brass trays, a dark wooden tray with a copper pin-holder cup in it, or treat yourself to a lovely "lotus" bowl at a Japanese shop. Use evergreen branches, iris, peonies (bud and full bloom), chrysanthemums, narcissuses, tulips, forsythias, dahlias. With just a few blooms and branches skillfully placed, you can make a stunning arrangement. You will not only be thrilled by the results, but you will also find it very easy on your pocketbook to have to buy only three or five flowers.

On page 64d there are illustrations showing you some examples of arrangements that you might like to see.

Know Your Containers

As YOU LOOK around your home you can probably think of a dozen places where you would like to see a flower arrangement. You know what a splash of color or a line of green would do for your living room. The small entrance hall with only a table and mirror in it could look double its size with a charming bowl of geraniums reflected in the mirror. Your bedroom could use a small bouquet of yellow mums to battle the dark winter skies outside.

Before you start, give some thought to the containers you will use. They contribute so much to the beauty and effectiveness of any arrangement.

Everybody has some containers! Vases of glass, metal, or porcelain—large ones for tall flowers or heavy shrubs, small ones for a single blossom; bowls that are just right for short-stemmed flowers. Drag them out from the shelf you keep them on, and look at them in a new light.

Are your containers merely functional? Or will they enhance the flowers and the greens you put into them and add to the beauty of your room? Is there enough variety in shape, color, and material to suit your decorating needs? For example, in a room decorated with bright and lively colors, you might want a green bowl to hold the flowers you have selected to match the reds and yellows in the slipcover. In a modern room a black or charcoal container would be handsome for your yellow tulips. Copper or brass matching urns with ivy in them would be stunning on either side of a Victorian mantelpiece. A bronze compote would be just the right container for the geraniums in the entrance hall. If you have a white bowl or vase, there should always be some white flowers or shrub blossoms in it to make a striking accent in the room.

The containers to hold your flowers are sometimes more important for decorating your home than the flowers themselves. A handsome reproduction of an Etruscan cup can be bought from the Metropolitan Museum of Art in New York City. It is tall, black, and has a 9-inch flaring cup on a 7-inch stem. It would lend its simple beauty to any flowers you chose: a stalk of the Martagon Album lily; simple white shasta daisies; short-stemmed marigolds or zinnias. Search antique shops or weekend auctions for brass or copper pitchers that would set off yellow and orange flowers.

Think of containers, too, in relation to the period of your furniture or the atmosphere you want to create. You are lucky if you have the bed and chest you grew up with to start your own family tradition. Perhaps you've found a charming dining-room table that you can afford in an antique shop. Or you may have invested in a handsome modern davenport and chair that will be the beginning of your special living style. Without realizing it, you will tend to collect containers that will echo the period of your furniture.

If you prefer a Colonial or Early American decor, try to find pewter teapots, pottery mugs, vases of saltglaze (old or new) to hold lilacs or forsythia; wooden knife boxes (lined with tin) to sit on your coffee table full of zinnias; glass bowls to hold roses in your living room. If you live in the city you may prefer the more formal eighteenth-century look of Williamsburg: a porcelain compote, old or new, on your dining-room table, with pink and yellow snapdragons; a crystal vase holding a mass of petunias in your living room.

At about this time in France there was a vogue for fruitwood chairs and tables, with charming printed chintz and linens as draperies and bedspreads. This decorating style, called French Provincial, is as comfortable and decorative for modern living as it was in eighteenth-century France. Containers of

brass, tôle (tin, painted in country patterns), wrought iron, pottery, and wood are appropriate for this period.

There are other distinctive styles of decorating in America's past that may interest you. The Amish, whose beautiful crafts are still visible on the barns of mid-Pennsylvania and New Glarus, Wisconsin, as well as on their quilts and bedspreads, painted chairs, and framed birth certificates, offer pewter, glass, and wooden objects to be used as containers. Their favorite flower was the tulip; their colors were flat red, scarlet, green, and yellow, with a touch of brown. So choose a deep red slipware vase and fill it with tulips, cherry branches, and tulip leaves, and use that as a "welcome" in your front hall.

Or an old wooden butter bowl arranged with bright gourds, hard squash, and red Indian corn would be an eye-catcher in your family room early in October. One of the first American glass factories was owned by "Baron" Stiegel in Lancaster County, Pennsylvania. You might find one of his diamond or reed-patterned glasses or pitchers on one of your antique hunts to fill with little 'Sweetheart' roses and English ivy at your next luncheon.

America is filled with the national heritages of other lands, too. The French and Spanish together in New Orleans have given us not only Creole cooking but Creole decoration: exquisite French porcelain, alabaster urns, delicate crystal vases. If you like this type of decoration, you don't have to barter your soul for the originals. Charming reproductions can be found in garage sales, auctions, even discount stores, if you look for them with a discerning eye. When you find them, all you need are some azaleas, violets, pansies, carnations, and blooms of clematis to create your own "plantation" arrangement.

The Victorian era has suddenly become a favorite style for many young people. They don't go all the way with horsehair couches or framed wax flowers, but the charming conch shells, the pressed-glass compotes and vases, the pale blue Parian glass twin vases with a hand clasping the center—all these are invitations to try to create an unusual arrangement. So many flowers and greens that you might use rush to mind: forget-me-nots, sweet williams, carnations, dahlias, blue salvia, ferns, peonies, and roses.

If you are interested in modern art, and you live happily with modern furniture, there is much in our Indian heritage to tempt you. The wonderful colors and textures of the patterns of the Southwest, with its Spanish and Mexican background, are primitive and irresistible. African primitive design, too, is compatible with a modern setting.

Did you ever realize that many containers that are effective in flower arranging were not created for that use? Just pick them out of their old niche and use your imagination. If your house and taste are formal, that little demitasse cup (with a hairline crack that makes its use for after-dinner coffee not feasible) would be charming on the guest-room table with delicate ageratum blossoms

in it (see page 48d). On your coffee table, a floating tuberous begonia would look elegant in a crystal brandy snifter. Even your tall silver candy dish would be a marvelous container for the delicate pink coral bells that bloom so madly in small rock gardens. There are probably hundreds of other possibilities in your cupboard, and only you would know about them.

If the decorating of your apartment or house is informal, pick up pieces in your kitchen: that red enameled teapot, or a colorful glass pitcher to hold summer snapdragons in your family room. (Don't forget that when you use a container with a spout or lip, you should have some blossoms or greens break over the lip or the spout.)

If you live in the country, put some giant sunflowers in that old umbrella stand you couldn't resist at the last auction. Bring your wooden salad bowl into the dining room filled with garden marigolds and yellow snapdragons.

If you are a haunter of antique shops or auctions, you can find fascinating objects to use as containers or as accessories with arrangements: pressed-glass vases, glasses,

or greens—a real conversation-stopper—or you ached to reach over and pull up the impossibly low flowers to give them some sense of proportion.

If you are having guests for dinner, with your best mats or cloth on parade, you might find that a compote, low or tall, would be the easiest thing for you to arrange. It could be of glass, silver, china, or pewter—anything stemmed that would give an air of elegance to your table. If your table is long, seating eight or ten guests, twin compotes would be perfect. You could then have flowers at both ends of the table. Either way, your guests wouldn't have to peek through the flowers to converse!

Remember that this arrangement has to be seen from both sides. Take a tall, light-colored, or small-budded flower as your center flower. Have it two and one-half times the height of your container. Pick out another flower, at least one-third shorter than the first, and fix it near the first. Pick out the third flower, much nearer the height of the second, and fix that on the other side of the first, still very close.

Now choose two flowers, also light and small-blossomed, and fix them, one on each side of the center, but stretching out as long sideways as the center flower does in height. Next choose two more flowers, shorter than the first, and fix them on each side of the first on both sides of the container, so that there are five flowers on each side, plus the three in the center.

Now your proportions are established. All you have to do is fill the spaces between top and sides, with the same or different flowers, using shorter and fuller blooms. Save the fullest blossoms, and the deepest-colored ones, for each side near the edge of the container.

For an informal luncheon or family dinner, any container with a stem is a godsend; but

cruets; cut-glass fruit bowls; little pressed-glass hats for miniature flowers; old glass pharmacy jars to hold long-stemmed blossoms; or, if you're lucky, the wonderful old ceramic jars with the names of their contents painted in Latin on the side. There are marvelous blue and white pottery salt holders with wooden covers that hinge upward, metal trays for modern arrangements, old glass kerosene lamps that can be filled with water when you screw the metal cover off. The world is your oyster! All you need is imagination, and you can have the most original containers in your town.

Even the most original decorator, however, must learn a few basic rules about choosing containers for the dinner table. Have you ever attended a luncheon or a dinner party and found yourself thinking unpardonable things about the flower arrangements on the table? Either you had to struggle to see the guest of honor through a tall mass of flowers now it can be of pottery or colored glass or an echo of your own figured china. You can devise one by turning one of your eggcups upside down and using Posey Klay to attach a large cereal bowl to it. An "instant" compote! Two more eggcups, padded with the clay to fit the base of a candle, give you a pair of candlesticks to match (see page 48d). Or other informal containers are acceptable: a brass bowl, round or square or oblong; twin wooden platters to hold fruit and flowers for a large crowd can combine decoration and dessert. A shallow bowl or even shallower tray can hold enough water for narcissuses or tulips. Or a cup pin holder can be used on a piece of driftwood and be hidden from sight by foliage, stones, or moss.

If you are planning a buffet supper or reception you might want to push your table close to the wall and use a lovely old soup tureen to hold a variety of flowers. Or, if you use both sides of your table, a wide modern glass bowl could hold three gladioluses at one end to balance the platters of meat and salad at the other.

You can often make an arrangement even more effective if you place it on a base. Watch for these handsome bases whenever you go to a flower show or join a house-and-garden tour. There are severe black Japanese stands, with feet, or the more ornate Chinese teak stands, cutout and elegant. You might find a modern white marble base on brass balls or a handsome polished slab of wood on which to set your Japanese-style arrangements. Or you can pick up a piece of driftwood at the beach or Victorian bases at the antique store. A base that enhances the beauty of your container will add distinction to your flower arrangements.

Once you have discovered or collected or invented your containers, try to find a special cupboard—or perhaps an old bookcase—with a couple of tall shelves where you can keep them. And, once you've discovered the efficient pin holder for a certain bowl, or have succeeded in crumpling up a mass of chicken wire that just fits in the neck of that troublesome vase which is the only one tall enough for delphiniums, *keep it there!* Make sure the clay underneath the pin holder is really Posey Klay and not a quick-stiffening substitute. Then be prepared to leave the pin holder there forever, even if it means going out and buying others when you need them for other containers. There's nothing more comforting, on a hectic day, than to know, when you pull out that bowl at the last minute before the guests arrive, that the pin holder is in there securely. Only then can you jab a top-heavy branch of flowering crabapple into it and know it won't fall over!

The Wonderful World
of Potted Plants

THERE IS another important source of living decorating material besides fresh flowers and greens: the world of potted plants. It literally encompasses the world, from Arctic to tropical jungle; it includes spring bulbs forced into bloom and desert cactuses that can live happily alone when you go away on vacation. Only a horticulturist would know them all! But if you know a few, and learn their tastes in light, sunshine, temperature, humidity, and water, you can increase your pleasure and double the beauty of your home.

You are the one to choose the plants you want. But try to hold yourself firmly in check and select only the number of plants you will have time to care for. Do you have a job? Do you have young children? Do you travel regularly, leaving no one at your home

to take charge? If so, start investing in plants cautiously until you find exactly which plants and how many you can handle.

LIGHT

Look at the light in your living room. Do the windows face the east? Does your bedroom have sunlight at least two hours a day? Is there a dark spot in your entrance hall that cries out for tall greenery? You are lucky if you are able to select potted plants that will live happily in every room.

An African violet, such as the lovely pale pink 'Lilian Jarrett' or any of the new double blossoms, will thrive in the cool light of an east window. So will wax begonia *(Begonia semperflorens),* and pots of English ivy *(Hedera helix).* And a lovely pink azalea will bloom

47

for weeks in the light of an east window. These are some blossoming plants that don't demand full sunlight. In rooms where south windows bring warm sunshine, you'll find a made-to-order spot for geraniums, a shrimp plant *(Beloperone guttata),* a group of coleus *(C. blumei)* in the new shades of white or avocado green, as well as fascinating succulents such as the echeverias. All you'll have to do is to turn your plants around every few days so that the leaves won't reach toward the sun and distort the plant's shape.

Chinese Evergreen

Geranium

Coleus

on a table or an 'Emerald Ripple' *(Peperomia capreata)* which will do well if there's moderate light. Some large potted plants will live happily in your living room with no windows near them.

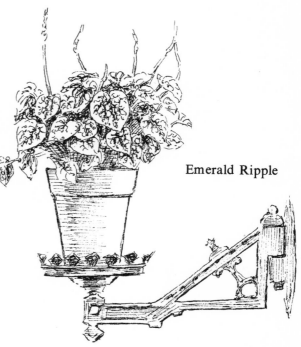

Emerald Ripple

But most foliage plants native to tropical jungle and the rain forests of Central America don't need strong sun. They will live comfortably near a north window or in the shadowy interior of a room. That means you can select a handsome pot of Chinese evergreen *(Aglaeonema modestum)* to grow in your entrance hall—on a table, if the plant is small; on the floor if it is tall. Or you can have a trailing kangaroo vine *(Cissus antarctica)*

Ideas for Summer

Summer offers its riches without any conditions. Take them all, use them recklessly. They will decorate your home with delight! June can bring weddings and lilies to celebrate them. Here in the hall of a stunning modern house is an arrangement of bowl-shaped 'Imperial Silver' lilies and Rubrum hybrids in an antique porcelain container. The greens are peony leaves.

ABOVE: *All periods of decoration blend well if they have excellent design. Proof: modern porcelain lavatory, Victorian mirror, antique glass bottle, Italian pottery soap dish and pots and hand-made "brick" flower container holding tall spare shasta daisies.*

RIGHT: *Antique handmade quilts are a decoration worthy of a matching flower arrangement. The container, an old Britanniaware teapot, holds two dozen small red roses, some spilling out toward the spout. Antique sugar bowl echoes the color, with an old Staffordshire pinbox next to it.*

48b

LEFT: *In August, flowers decorate your outdoor living. This fat strawberry jar on the terrace wall bulges with white 'Cascade' petunias, pink begonias 'Linda', yellow pansies 'Pay Dirt', blue ageratums topped with coral geraniums. Two baskets of pink Elatior begonias hang from the crabapple tree. In the background, phlox, lilies, and marigolds.*

BELOW: *Buffet Sunday dinner on the terrace. Pale green Italian cloth, plates, and mugs. Two tall copper containers hold white false dragonhead* (Dracocephalum virgianum), *'Enchantment' lilies, and pink snapdragons. Fruit arranged in the center provides dessert.*

ABOVE: *'Instant compote': from eggcup and bowl.*
Candlesticks from other eggcups!
Yellow snapdragons and blue cornflowers.

ABOVE: *Black reproduction Etruscan bowl from*
the Metropolitan Museum of Art in New York.
White false dragonhead, zinnias.

LEFT: *Victorian pitcher, hand-painted, of charming*
style and color. Arrangement of green bells of Ireland
(Molucella laevis), two shades of red zinnias.
Brown pitcher in background.

BELOW: *Miniature arrangement in blue and gold*
demitasse. White cosmos, pink begonias 'Linda',
ageratums, pansies. Set on carved base.
Antique Austrian demitasse at right.

TEMPERATURE

Not only light but temperature helps you decide what potted plants to use to decorate your home. Most plants thrive in 62°–70° F., preferring 55°–60° at night. But many human beings prefer a little more heat than that, unless they live in Zone 6 or farther south, where winter does not bring zero and below-zero temperatures outside. If your home is set for 70° or a little more, make sure the plants you choose can "take it." All the succulents that come from the desert are very much at home in the temperatures of most American homes. Most flowering plants love the sun from fall to spring, though they have to be shielded from it in summer. Those plants that demand 50°–60° temperatures in the daytime should either be housed on a cool, enclosed porch or in your own greenhouse. But most foliage plants, tender bulbs, and the hardy spring bulbs are happy to share your pleasant temperature.

HUMIDITY

The problem many plant lovers have to solve is not the heat but the humidity. Your house or apartment may not only be hot, but it may be dry. English ivy, Chinese evergreen, and kangaroo vine *(Cissus antarctica)* need moist soil—as do begonias and African violets. A small hygrometer can tell you the humidity of your room. If it is about 40–60 percent you might find that a small portable electric humidifier would make you as happy as it would your plants. Or you can spray your potted plants regularly over the sink with a small atomizer spray; this will refresh the foliage as well as keep it clean and healthy. There are many tricks to watering your potted plants that will raise the humidity around them and not require either time or expense to you.

The easiest method is setting your plants in a metal tray on top of ½ inch of small

Kangaroo Vine

pebbles which can be watered each morning. This makes the humidity rise. The water in the potted plants drains into the pebbles to create moisture. If there is no tray under the plants, set each plant into a larger pot with small stones at the bottom. When they're watered, the extra moisture will settle around the plants without getting their feet too damp.

On pages 142–152 you will find a chart of house plants listed alphabetically by their common names, with the light, temperature and humidity requirements of each. You

Jade Plant

should know whether your plant needs sun, prefers only medium light, or doesn't need any light in order to place it properly. You should also know whether you can supply the light, temperature, and humidity requirements for the plants you might like to own. If a plant you want is not listed, ask your florist to advise you about its needs.

One more practical consideration before you select your plants: select some varieties that will have a double use. For instance, a simple green foliage plant such as the jade plant *(Crassula argentea)* in a charming green pottery bowl will thrive in your living room on the coffee table, but can also make a pleasant centerpiece for an informal luncheon, or be whisked to the guest room for an unexpected overnighter. Or a blooming pink cyclamen *(C. persicum)* that will last for weeks in your family room, near an east window, can also grace the entrance hall or a buffet-dinner table, and go back to the family room whenever you want it.

A tall potted "tree" will live happily in the darkest corner of your living room, requiring only water and an occasional washing of its leaves. If some of these trees are unknown to you, go to your favorite greenhouse and

get acquainted. There's dumbcane *(Dieffenbachia picta)* or a handsome fiddle-leaf fig *(Ficus lyrata)* or a Chinese evergreen *(Aglaeonema modestum)* or dracaena *(Dracaena deremensis),* with green stripes down its long, pale green leaves. All these tall plants may be a little more expensive than the small jade tree, but they'll be yours forever and will grow and grow.

Please don't become impatient with these strange Latin names for ordinary green plants. Long ago, the brilliant botanist Carl Linneaus spent a great deal of time gathering every flower, grass, and weed he could find in his native Sweden and then spent years sorting them into families, which he then named. He named them in Latin so they could be understood by botanists all over the world. If you know the Latin name of

Fiddle-leaf Fig

the potted plants you own, as well as the flowers or greens you buy, you are on your way to becoming a botanist too. But for most people, the common names suffice.

Dracena

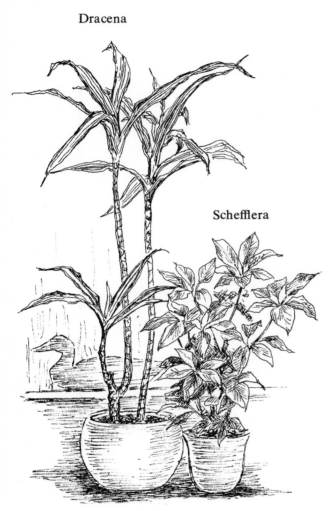

Schefflera

Decorating with Plants

How can potted plants serve you as a decorating device? Besides answering your need for living greens and blossoms, plants, like flowers, can add color to complement your living-room curtains or contrast with the monotone of your modern bedroom.

POTS AND CONTAINERS

The containers of plants become as important in your home as the plants themselves. The period of your furniture, or the overall decor of your room, can be highlighted by the choice of the container.

There was a time when old-fashioned clay pots were considered to be the best containers for plants. But most horticulturists agree that plastic or polyethylene pots, with drainage holes in the base, are equally as good and preferable for many reasons.

Most plastic pots are cheaper than clay pots. They don't dry out as fast as clay, so plants stay moist longer. They aren't as heavy to lift or carry. They are much less vulnerable, if they happen to be dropped or hit each other. New clay pots must be soaked in water overnight and then allowed to dry completely. Otherwise they will draw water from the plants that are potted in them. Plastic pots have a smooth finish and can be rinsed quickly with water; clay pots, once used, must be scrubbed with a stiff brush and hot water to remove the crusted soil inside.

Although large hand-molded clay pots with curving rims are stunning, they are quite expensive. Ordinary large plastic pots are more reasonably priced. However, plastic pots molded to look like bamboo or woven straw are equal in price to the handmade clay pots. You must be the judge of what you want and how much you are willing to spend.

Containers for potted plants are made of many unusual materials today. There are handmade ceramic containers with Mexican ornaments, or designs copied from Italian Renaissance molds; rough, woven-grass containers, cocoa and deep brown; stunning glasslike pots, made of plastic; and Japanese wooden tubs, lined with metal. The periods of your furnishings and the origin of the plant should guide you in choosing the appropriate container.

If you have a collection of fancy-leaved geraniums or small herbs, or a window of glass shelves filled with pots of African violets, try putting each plant in the same color square plastic pot. It could be pale green, or shocking pink, or yellow, or white. When the collection is dressed in identical colors it will give the accent you need. Look on page 96a at the dwarf geraniums in pink pots, set on pebbles in a copper tray. On a large windowsill, with pale white curtains framing them, they not only blend with the color of the woodwork but also show off the beauty of the lovely plants.

Aeonium

A country house with Early American feeling would welcome pewter containers for geraniums, ivy, or African violets. A modern apartment would look smart with a handsome succulent plant (perhaps *Aeonium* or *Echeveria*) in a glazed or unglazed bowl or pot— the kind used for growing "Bonzai" trees. If you are interested in the kind of decor found in Arizona or Southern California, you might choose a Spanish pottery container or a redwood pot. If you love the Victorian era, you'll find charming pottery bowls, made originally to hold Boston fern, but just as at home with your wax begonia or pale pink azaleas. All you need do is keep your eyes open, look at all the handsome houses open at flower-show tours, or take out a book on antiques from the library, and let your imagination do the rest.

Plants as Architectural Aids

There is another way in which handsome, well-grown plants can serve your decorating needs as flower arrangements cannot. They can turn you into an "instant architect"!

Are you living in a modern, open-spaced apartment that must use one room for living-dining-cooking areas? Many people are. But you can divide that one room into three with a few potted plants: a tall dumbcane *(Dieffenbachia picta)* and fiddle-leaf fig *(Ficus lyrata)* plus a shorter Chinese evergreen *(Aglaeonema modestum)* grouped together between your living-room chairs and your dropleaf dining table. They will make a green, living divider in an otherwise cluttered room. The plants won't add to the clutter. They don't demand sunlight—just water and Tender Loving Care.

Between dining and cooking areas there are other ways to use plants as a divider. If there's a counter for preparing the food, that would be a fine place for potted herbs: parsley, garlic chives, English thyme, tarragon—plus a sturdy pot of aloe in case you burn your fingers at the stove. (*Aloe variegata* is one of the medicinal herbs you should always have in the kitchen. It is a succulent —strange, pale olive green with fat, juicy pointed branches. If you touch a hot pan or get a drop of hot grease on your hand, break off a bit of the aloe, pull it open, and put it on the burn. A Band-Aid will hold it in place, and the pain will be gone instantly. The burned spot will not blister or get infected or even *hurt!)* If there is a divided counter between the kitchen and dining areas, the pots of herbs can be placed on the dining-room side of the counter, with trailing ivy between the herb pots to emphasize the imaginary division into two rooms. The herb pots can be whisked away to a sunny window every other day if they show signs of needing it. Or they may have two long tubes of Gro-Lux fastened above them so that they think they are living in tropical sunlight!

Suppose, instead of being forced to make three rooms out of one, you are faced with the opposite problem. You have rented a lovely old house with a living room so large, it needs twice as much furniture as you possess to fill it. How can your potted plants help you here?

Turn half of your living room into a garden. Group your couch, desk, chairs, tables, lamps at one end of the room and fill the front end, near the windows, with all the plants you can possibly afford. Some can be tall: a "tree" of weeping fig *(Ficus benjamina),* which takes indirect light, placed away from the window, or a tall blossoming hibiscus, which can take sun all year round. Some plants can be small, set in copper trays on two-stepped plant stands. Or there are old wicker planters that will hold three or four ferns spilling over the edge. If you have inherited a tea cart, you can use the two shelves for collections of scented geraniums and can wheel them from sun to shade. If your room is modern, use tall polyethylene cubes, smoky brown or milky white, to hold a special

Weeping Fig

calamondin orange plant in a straw cache pot. With imagination you can arrange all heights and sizes in special groupings, according to their need for light, their texture, their compatibility. A long-spouted watering can will reach the clustered plants.

All this will not cost a quarter of the price of a new chair. You will derive great pleasure from living with these substitute furnishings, and you will find that they are real conversation pieces.

If the ceiling is too high—as it is in many old houses—hanging baskets can create an architectural illusion. One or two (spider plant or coleus or wandering Jew) hanging from brackets at the window will break the large area of empty space and will actually minimize the height of the ceiling.

Plants can serve another practical purpose. Many modern houses have two or three levels. There may be two steps down from the dining room to the living room; or three steps from a sun room to a terrace. There is always the haunting fear that someone will not realize that the steps are there and possibly fall. A sturdy potted plant near the top step —a tall schefflera with three small, softening pots of fern around it will serve as a warning. It might help to train a Gro-Lux on this plant, not only to give it extra light to grow but to make sure that everyone sees it.

Seasonal Plants

Potted plants can be changed with the seasons. At Christmas there are deep rose azaleas, white cyclamen, orangy-red Jerusalem cherry *(Solanum pseudocapsicum),* bright kalanchoes with leathery leaves and brick red flowers as well as the familiar Christmas cactus *(Schlumbergera bridgesii)* and the bright-green pepper plant *(Capsicum annuum).* Or the exquisite Riegor Elatior begonia in deep pink or yellow and white that can hang in a basket as a special holiday beauty. And of course, the decorative poinsettias, which come in white and pink, as well as Christmas red, and last so long you may be tired of looking at them by February! Give them to your

Amaryllis

Christmas
Cactus

best friends and next Christmas give yourself a marvelous amaryllis, from which you will get at least two stalks with four, maybe five, glorious blossoms. They will last five or six weeks, then you will have a lovely green plant which in summer can be set outside until fall. When you bring it in, set it in the garage or the basement or a dark closet without water until it is completely dry and the foliage turns yellow. Then cut the foliage off, turn it on its side, and wait patiently until you see little green leaves starting again. Take it up, put it in a warm spot, water it, and you will have glorious blossoms all over again by Christmas! Look on page 96d to see a red- and white-striped amaryllis still blooming on Washington's Birthday.

Have you ever thought of decorating your fireplace in spring and summer when it is no longer needed for open fires? A charming method is to pile armloads of green *Magnolia grandiflora* branches in the fireplace, face them with three pots of *Aeonium*, which require little water in summer and whose pale color is an interesting contrast to the magnolia leaves. As the weeks go by, the magnolia leaves will darken; by fall, when you need the fireplace again, they will be a lovely color for you to put into another arrangement somewhere else. Look at the potted plants you have in your house or your florists' collection for other ideas to make your empty fireplace a decorative addition to your room.

In the fall, try putting two pots of short-stemmed chrysanthemums into an indoor window box with three green ivy plants trailing over the sides, or jade plants, or two small pots of podocarpus to give you an evergreen contrast. When the mums have lost their blossoms, replace them with Jerusalem cherry for the winter, or shrimp plant or two shades of coleus, to give you Christmas color for the holidays. And when the holiday season is over and you are longing for the soothing effect of white or pale blue or yellow, find another spot for the holiday colors and put hyacinths in their place. Later, substitute narcissuses or tulips, all potted beauties which you may have forced yourself the previous fall. If you don't have bulbs, use the azalea someone sent you for Christmas—hopefully pale pink or white. Or treat yourself to a blooming pot of calceolaria, yellow and orange or blue and white; put it in the center of your window box and let all the greens on either side just minister to it. Before you know it, spring is here. And it's time for potted geraniums, potted petunias, potted lobelias—maybe the whole box can be filled with solid potted white alyssum which could (might!) live there happily all summer long.

All you have to do is make sure that there is an inch of small gravel on the bottom of the box and that all the pots have good drainage holes. It might be a good idea to have the pots raised from the gravel an inch or two with metal canning rings. That way, none of the greens or flowers will get too wet.

Kentia Palm

Madagascar and needs strong light, though not necessarily sun. It is graceful and will make your living room very handsome. Then there's the lady palm *(Rhapis excelsa),* which is different from the others. It grows slowly —you can rarely find one taller than 3 or 4 feet—but you can put it anywhere in your house if there is some light. It will be interesting to find these trees at your local conservatory or look for them in that special book from the library.

From trees it may seem a long trail back to the little green bowl of jade plant *(Crassula argentea)* that might have been your first purchase of a potted plant. But it is only a matter of size. All plants need the same things: water, light, soil, humidity—and a container. It is up to you to find out enough about each plant to be able to give it what it needs.

Trees—The Elegant Potted Plants

After you have had some experience with potted plants, you might decide to purchase a sizable "tree" for your family room or your living room. You already know the fiddle-leaf fig and the schefflera. But have you thought of having one in a 12-inch box, reaching almost 5 feet tall? There are palm trees that would be handsome in your house, too. Of these, Kentia palm *(Howeia forsteriana)* is the hardiest of all. It will grow in sun or poor light, does not attract insects, and will not be set back if you go away and let it be dry for days at a time. There's the cane, or butterfly palm *(Chrysalidocarpus lutescens).* This plant is native to

Lady Palm

How to Care for
Your Potted Plants

WATERING

Don't drown your plants. They don't all have to be watered every day. You will find that plants in plastic pots need watering less frequently than those in clay pots. Moisture from the soil passes through porous clay just as outside air passes through clay to the soil. This cannot happen in a plastic pot, which is not porous. When the top of the soil in a clay pot looks dry and feels dry to your fingertips, you know it is dry all the way through and needs a really deep drink until the water runs out of the drainage hole in the bottom of the pot.

Not so with plastic. There the moisture stays almost twice as long as it does in soil potted in clay. The surface of the soil is not a good indication of the dryness beneath it. You will have to thrust your finger or a small stick down about 2 inches to see whether or not the moisture is gone. If you give your plant more water while it is still moist, the poor roots will begin to sicken and die. This happens because an excess of water pushes the oxygen out of the soil, and oxygen is not only necessary to the fine roots, but also keeps the soil in good condition. All you have to remember is that plants in plastic pots stay moist twice as long as plants in clay pots.

No matter what kind of pot you use, your plant must not sit in a little pool after it's watered. If there is water in the saucer under the pot after you water the plant, drain it. If you place a small layer of pebbles under the pot, the water will not accumulate under the plant, but will be evaporated by the warm air around it. Try to water all your pots and boxes in the morning, when the temperature is rising. If the day is gloomy and cloudy,

don't water at all that day. Fill the watering can before you go to bed, so the water is room temperature by morning when it reaches your plants. This is particularly important for African violets, which do not like cold water. They don't like wet leaves, either. In fact, it is advisable to water all plants without splashing the foliage.

When a plant is dormant, that is, resting and not actively growing, give it less water than you would ordinarily. The dormant period is different for all varieties of plants from bulbs to foliage trees, depending on where their great-grandparents originally grew. It's easy to know when hardy bulbs such as hyacinths, narcissuses, and tulips are dormant. They are in that stage when you purchase them, and whether you put them outside in a border or force them inside in a pot, you know they must have from three to six months to rest, form their roots, and develop into a plant ready to flower. Tender tubers such as dahlias, tuberous begonias, and bulbs of amaryllis must have a dormant period, in or out of the earth, to rest for the next season. But it is often harder to recognize dormancy in other plants. Azaleas, chrysanthemums, geraniums, and African violets all come from tropical lands. If you purchase them in the "bud stage" they will last much longer than they will if you buy them in full bloom. Put the mums and geraniums in warm sunlight, the azaleas and African violets in cool light. Give them generous waterings and feedings as they prepare to bloom, but restrict both the water and food when they are in full flower. When the blooms are gone, the plants are ready for their rest and don't need much water. The succulent plants, though they are not desert plants, prepare to rest during the winter months also. Their leaves are torpid, and when they are dormant demand very little water since they draw on their own moisture. The foliage plants, even

57

the tall "tree forms," are mostly from tropical zones and definitely need a rest from watering or feeding when they are dormant in the winter months. When spring comes you can see a quickening of new growth, which is a signal to increase their watering and give them a balanced fertilizer.

FEEDING

Feeding your house plants is not a difficult task. The simplest, most effective method is to purchase fertilizer that's made to be dissolved in water. All plants need the same three major nutrients—nitrogen, phosphorus, potassium—plus small amounts of minor or "trace" minerals. Most modern complete soluble fertilizers also contain vitamins and hormones to provide the plants with everything they need. They come in high analysis and in different proportions, always with the ingredients listed in the same order (nitrogen, phosphorus, potassium). "High analysis" means there is more of each ingredient concentrated in a small amount of this soluble fertilizer. This kind of fertilizer is more expensive because some of the ingredients, such as the instantly soluble phosphates, are higher in cost. But, to the home gardener, they are worth their price. They are easy to mix with water, they won't burn the plant, and they can be bought in small quantities without waste. Make sure, of course, that your plant needs food. In winter, or in the plant's "rest period," it doesn't need fertilizer. In spring, when new leaves appear, it would like a high-nitrogen food, such as 10-6-4. If it is a flowering plant, give it a fertilizer with a high phosphorous content, such as 5-10-5 or 15-30-15. If it is a large foliage plant originally from a tropical climate, and it is as healthy and as high as you want it, you might not want to fertilize it at all. Otherwise a fertilizer of 15-15-30 would provide potassium

for strong root formation and resistance to disease. Be sure you choose the proper preparation for the proper plants. Read the directions carefully on the box of fertilizer and dilute it exactly as the maker suggests. The fertilizer may be applied to your plants every two weeks. Be sure the soil is not dry when you apply it. Don't feed the high-nitrogen formula to geraniums or azaleas. If you do, the foliage will outstrip the flowers. If you are interested in "foliar feeding"—spraying a less concentrated solution of the fertilizer directly on the leaves of the plant—read the directions on the package carefully to be sure your plants can be fed in this way. Sometimes two or three weekly foliar feedings will improve the looks and health of a plant tremendously. Then you can go back to regular feedings through the soil. (See chart on pages 142–152 for instructions for watering and fertilizing each plant mentioned.)

INSECT CONTROL

Watch your plants carefully to see whether they have been visited by those unwelcome visitors most plants are heir to. There are two groups of pests with which you will have to deal. The "chewing pests" actually eat the leaves of your plants leaving holes or brown spots, cutting off stems, making leaves roll under. These include small green caterpillars, nematodes, slugs, and cutworms. The only way to defeat them is with a "stomach poison," which you must apply like a special sauce to their favorite leaves.

The second group—the "sucking pests"—pierce the foliage of plants and suck the juices from inside the leaves and stems. No invitation is needed for them to find your lovely plants! There seems to be an unbreakable code that alerts these enemies to the fact that you have joined the list of humans who provide them with food. Because they don't eat the leaves they must be killed by a "contact poison." Three of these insects are so minute they can hardly be seen. If you look carefully underneath new tender shoots you can see the tiny aphids— yellow, green, or black—that will busily destroy the leaves. If the plants are a reasonable size and not flowering, you might be able to wash the aphids down the kitchen drain: cover the surface of the soil with aluminum paper and dunk the leaves into sudsy water in the kitchen sink. But this is hardly the method to use on a blooming begonia or a tall fiddle-leaf fig!

Cyclamen mites are invisible in themselves but not in their work. Like aphids, they feed (by sucking) on new growth, which will appear twisted and misshapen. The leaves never grow to full size; they stay small and finally fall off.

Red spider, or two-spotted spider mite, is another sucking insect that attacks the underside of tender new growth. The leaves become mottled and brown and die if you let the insects multiply. These insects are only visible under a magnifying glass, but you can discover their presence by the fine web they spin, which will cover the whole plant if you don't eradicate them. They love dry air without proper humidity. A fine washing or misting of small plants over the kitchen sink can give some protection.

The only real protection from these pests comes from regular, faithful spraying. The quickest, simplest way is to use an aerosol spray can which contains a "contact poison" such as Malathion or Zectran plus a "stomach poison" such as Methoxichlor or Sevin. If you are opposed to using aerosol spray cans because of the possible danger of the propellant to our ozone layer, it is simple and economical to mix your own insecticide and use it in your own sprayer. The following formula is excellent for both kinds of insects, plus fungus diseases:

To ½ gallon of water add:
1 teaspoon 50% Malathion spray (contact poison)
1 tablespoon 50% Methoxichlor wettable powder (stomach poison)
1 tablespoon Ferban 76% wettable powder (for fungus diseases)

Stir vigorously until all ingredients are completely dissolved, then pour into the sprayer. Store any leftover solution in a marked glass jar, tightly covered, out of the reach of children.

Of all the sucking pests the mealybug is the most maddening. It looks like an innocent speck of white cotton in the branch of a leaf. Don't be deceived! Get yourself a bottle of wood alcohol, a box of toothpicks, and some cotton. Twist a tiny piece of cotton on the end of the toothpick, dip it in the alcohol, and touch the mealybug with it. That will be the end of that! Of course if it is a large infestation, the whole plant must be sprayed with Malathion, either from an aerosol spray or by mixing ¾ teaspoon of 50% Malathion to 1 quart water. The mealybug is one of three scale insects that damage ornamental plants by sucking. A second pest is called armored scale; the third, soft scale. Both secrete a waxy covering that makes them look like part of the plant. All three excrete large amounts of "honeydew," which provides a medium for growth of a black fungus called sooty mold. This is unsightly but usually disappears when the insects are killed.

A sucking pest that you may never see on your plants is called simply what it is: whitefly. It lives in constantly increasing numbers beneath every leaf of the plant. You may not know it is there until you touch the branch or blossom and see literally hundreds of small white flies rise like a storm cloud before your eyes. Even in a greenhouse they are almost impossible to conquer—except with three or four continuous days of spraying. If you have these whiteflies on a small or medium-size plant or on a blooming specimen that you feel you could sacrifice, you would be wise to get rid of the plant at once, before all your plants are infected. It is not worth the risk to try to kill whiteflies. If you feel you cannot sacrifice your plant, spray it at once with an aerosol bomb or your own mixture, then call the florist or the nearest garden shop to ask advice. There are special "whitefly killer" chemicals advertised by seed houses such as George J. Ball, Inc., West Chicago, Illinois 60185; George W. Park Seed Co., Greenwood, South Carolina 29647; and W. Atlee Burpee Co., Clinton, Iowa 52732. These are labeled "All Ages," meaning that they will kill the eggs and the young flies as well as the old.

With good luck, and a watchful eye on all your plants, you can get rid of most unwelcome visitors. A regular treatment with an all-purpose spray every two weeks will bring you and your plants the best luck of all.

GROOMING

Another important way to keep your homebound garden really decorative is to keep it well groomed. If your plants have flowers, remove each withered blossom when its petals droop. If the plant is reaching up too high and not branching out to make more blooms, "top" it off a bit. This means heartlessly pruning back the overlong center stalk. The plant will then throw out some side branches to take its place. Soon more blooms will appear, and the shape of the plant will be much improved. If leaves fall off a plant, pick them up from pot, table, or floor. If the edge of a leaf turns ragged or brown, strip off the leaf, if it is small, or carefully trim the edges back to healthy green, if they are large, decorative leaves

that are too important to lose. Then find out why the leaves are browning and hasten to correct the trouble! It may be insects on the plant; too little or too much light; lack of fertilizer, particularly nitrogen. Or it may be the plant is potbound and needs to be moved to a larger container. Or there may be too much sun burning the leaves. Foliage plants often collect dust on the surface of their leaves which blocks normal transpiration. Large leaves can be washed off gently with a cloth dipped in water to make them shiny and green again. Small foliage plants can actually be dunked head down in clear water to clean them. Let the plant dry thoroughly before you put it back in the sunlight. A small metal rake (called an "indoor cultivator") sold in garden supply stores will be handy for shallow cultivation of the soil in the pot to keep it fresh-looking. If you don't have one of these small rakes, you can use an old fork.

REPOTTING

In fact, with all the conditions necessary for raising beautiful plants to decorate your home—the right temperature, humidity, light, and fertilizer plus keeping them groomed and healthy—some of them are going to respond so heartily that you'll see them bulging out of the tops of their pots or discover that their white roots are reaching out of the drainage hole in the bottom. These are signals that your plant needs a larger container.

If you have a garden, and if it is the time of year when you can go outdoors to get some soil, just dig some up. But if you have to buy soil, there are bags of it waiting for you at the florist or any gardening shop or variety store. You can use regular potting soil as it comes to you, because it will have all the necessary food in it. Or you can "improve" the commercial soil by adding your own components: more humus, to help it hold water longer, and your own sand or perlite or vermiculite, to make it more "friable" and easily crumbled.

The humus can be chopped sphagnum moss or peat moss, both available where you bought the soil. Be sure to wet the moss thoroughly before you add it to the prepared soil. If it is not wet before you mix it, you will have problems with it. One method is to pour boiling water over it, then (when the moss is not too hot) wring the water out again. For most plants, equal parts of prepared soil, peat moss, and perlite or sharp sand or vermiculite will be perfect. But then, to make sure the fertilizer is in proper proportions to this "improved" soil, add some steamed bonemeal to each pot—about 1 teaspoonful to a 6-inch pot. This is an organic fertilizer that will not burn the fine roots of the plant. It should be put near the bottom of the pot to draw the roots down to it. If you are repotting cactuses or succulent plants that don't need much water, you can use two parts prepared mix and one part each of peat moss and perlite or sand.

If you have never repotted a plant, you will get the knack quickly. Make sure you have an open space to work and that your soil is already mixed. Have your new pot ready, too, which means that it is scrubbed clean and dried out again, that you have shards (broken pieces of clay pot) or one of the plastic, circular 1½-inch drainage covers over the drainage hole of a clay pot, plus 1 inch of pebbles in the bottom of a plastic pot. Now, take the plant that needs to be transplanted, turn it upside down with its stem fastened safely between the middle fingers of your left hand, and tap the bottom of the pot sharply. The plant should drop out easily from its old home!

Put some soil into the new pot, add the steamed bonemeal, then set your plant into

it. There should be at least 1 inch around the edge of the plant for you to fill with soil. Use a thin stick to tap the soil into the pot gently, then bang the pot on the table to settle the soil and fill up any air pockets. Fill the pot with soil, up to 1 inch of the top. Give the plant a drink (unless it is a succulent which prefers dry soil at first), wash the remains of the operation off the pot (and yourself), and your lovely plant is ready to go back to your room again.

PROPAGATION

There's always the possibility, of course, that when you look at the swelling size of the plant you're going to repot, you may realize that you don't want it in a larger pot after all. There's enough of that healthy plant to fill two pots of the same size that you have now.

You have now entered a fascinating branch of horticulture known as *propagation:* the methods of increasing your supply of plants from your own stock. There are several ways this can be done, all of them easy and economical:

Division, which you can do when the plant is large enough.

Rooting, which you can do by taking a cutting or a leaf from an old plant to root and produce another plant just like it.

Layering, which you can do to large foliage plants that have grown too long and skinny.

Sowing, which you can do by planting new seeds to create new plants.

Division. This is the swiftest, simplest method. First make sure your plant is "divisible"—that it has two or three separate sections that you can pull or cut apart with sufficient root system for each. Have the new pot ready (scrubbed and crocked if it's a used clay pot; washed and an inch of gravel over the drainage holes if it's plastic) and the proper soil near at hand. Remove the large plant from its outgrown home, feel gently where the division could come, and carefully separate the one large plant into two smaller ones. If it will not separate easily with your fingers, you will have to operate, which means slicing it through bravely with a sharp knife that you have

sterilized in a solution of laundry bleach. Hold the half-plant in the new pot with one hand while you sift the prepared soil gently around and over the roots until it is safely set into its new home. Firm it down with both hands until it is settled at the same height it had been growing before. Then put the pot in your kitchen sink while you water it and attend to repotting the other half of the old plant into its original pot where, it is to be hoped, it will fit perfectly now!

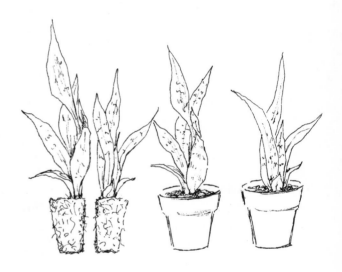

Rooting. Rootings are not so swiftly accomplished but are quite satisfying. Sometimes you may have an especially handsome geranium (e.g., 'Carefree, Deep Salmon') which blooms bountifully in your sun room, or a lovely potted begonia (like the silver- and green-leaved 'It' with pink blossoms). Both these plants are F_1 Hybrids, which makes them expensive to buy, but both are simple to reproduce by rooting. (F_1 is a hybrid strain developed from two parent plants that have desirable characteristics. The seed reverts back to one parent the next year, so there is no use saving seeds to plant another season. You won't get the flower you want.)

For your begonia you must have a 6-inch bulb pan cleaned out, crocked, and filled with a rooting medium. Again you may choose perlite, vermiculite, or a combination of sharp sand and peat moss or sphagnum moss, all of which, when moistened, are ideal for promoting new roots. To hurry these roots along, buy a small container of hormone powder (Hormodin #1 or Rootone) and make sure you have a sharp, clean knife for your surgery. To root the geranium, clean, crock, or gravel a 3-inch clay or plastic pot and fill it with a regular growing soil (from your garden or bought) up to ½ inch of the top. Then take a clean teaspoon, scoop out 1½ inches of the soil in the center, and replace it with the rooting medium you have chosen. Dampen the medium in both pots so that it is moist but not soggy.

Now you are ready. Choose a medium-aged branch of the begonia and geranium. This will root more easily than a frail new growth. Cut each branch about 3 to 4 inches long, just below a node, where other leaves will begin to grow. Remove all buds or blooms from the cutting as well as any leaves near the end of the stem. Dip the cut end of the begonia cutting in the hormone powder. Gently shake off any excess. Put the begonia into the medium in the bulb pan deep enough for it to stand securely. Firm it down.

Let the geranium cutting dry out for an hour, then dust the cut end with the hormone and insert it in the rooting medium in the 3-inch pot. Do not let the cut end reach beyond the rooting medium into the soil.

Slip each pot into a plastic bag held up from the leaves of the rootings by two thin sticks or plant markers. Then put the pots on a shelf above a radiator or set them on an electric heating pad turned to "low" to speed up the rooting process. Don't put them in direct sun. Keep them shaded a

day or two with a folded newspaper resting on top of the plastic covering. After that time, all you have to do is take off the plastic every couple of days and mist the cuttings to be sure the medium remains moist. In about a week or ten days, roots will be growing on both cuttings.

You can transplant the new begonia plant into its own 3-inch pot, water it, and set it in the light to grow.

The geranium will find all the food and soil it needs below the rooting medium. You won't have to do anything to the new plant but put it in the sunlight and watch it develop. This easy method of rooting geraniums was invented by Edith Farwell of Lake Forest, Illinois, much to the delight of the young beginning gardeners to whom she told her secret.

You'll discover many of your plants will root as easily as begonias and geraniums: coleus, impatiens, chrysanthemums, fuchsias, wandering Jew. The woody-stemmed plants —azalea, wax plant *(Hoya),* shrimp plant— even the miniature orange and lemon trees can be reproduced by cuttings. These are called "hardwood cuttings" and will need a Hormodin #3 rooting compound to help them. These take longer than the softwood cuttings, but they will grow roots if you are patient.

Rooting can be accomplished with a leaf as well as a branch in some plants like African violets, peperomias, and large Rex begonias. Be sure the African violet leaf has a short stem (petiole) on it, thrust it into the Hormodin, then into the moist rooting medium. Keep it warm, out of strong light,

and covered with a plastic bag to conserve its moisture. In a few weeks you will see little leaves showing above the surface, which will tell you the new plants are ready to be transplanted into their own new pots. A large Rex begonia leaf with its colored veins showing likes to be laid flat on the moist rooting medium. With the tip of a sharp knife, cut across those veins in three or four places, then pin the leaf down with tiny loops of wire so that it touches the medium.

Keep this pot warm and moist under a plastic cover, and you will soon see little baby plants appear along the slashes. Wait until they seem quite strong. Give them a well-diluted feeding of the 15–15–30 fertilizer to strengthen the developing roots about once a week. When they begin to look like new little Rex begonia plants, you can cut them loose from the leaf and pot each one in its own little 3-inch pot.

Ideas for Fall

Autumn's beauty is overpowering. Flowers, trees, shrubs, and vegetables glow with rich color outside. Bring some inside your home. This warm country game room has walls of used barn wood. An old wicker birdcage is draped with bittersweet vine. Antique umbrella stand holds dried allium, cattails, wheat. Huge copper maple-syrup kettle is filled with pumpkins, squash, gourds, corn.

ABOVE: *Elegant library. Hand-carved Italian marble fireplace with handsome antique glass screen. Arrangements on each side of gold mirror. Vases: German porcelain with gold handles. Flowers: small white button chrysanthemums; pale gold and deep bronze peony leaves.*

RIGHT: *Guest room. Hand-painted yellow Provincial dresser, with eighteenth-century Sheraton shaving mirror in center. On each side, antique Parian vases holding yellow roses and baby's breath.*

64b

LEFT: *Handsome deep-blue Staffordshire tureen on stone arch of staircase. Three glycerinized magnolia branches (pale beige); five huge Fuji chrysanthemums with deep brown magnolia leaves at base. Arrangement placed on cutout teakwood stand.*

BELOW: *Large, charming room divided into living and dining areas by potted plants. Four tall potted trees behind couch. Brass pole from floor to ceiling with hanging baskets:* wax plant (Hoya carnosa), *episcia,* kangaroo vine (Cissus antarctica), *and* burro-tailed sedum (Sedum morganianum).

STEP-BY-STEP INSTRUCTION FOR TWO LOVELY FLOWER ARRANGEMENTS.

1. *All materials ready: pale and d[ark] chrysanthemums, lavender and dar[k] purple asters, scissors, container.*

2. *Start with pale mums, tall (2½ times height of container), wi[th] small blossoms at top and right side of arrangement.*

3. *Add pale asters at center and t[all] in profile at rear.*

4. *Add dark mums, small at edge[s,] large in center. Add dark asters.*

5. *Complete with dark asters at b[ase.]*

1. *Two dozen 'Sonia' roses. Silver bowl filled with oasis; water; sciss[ors.] Mass arrangement to be seen from all sides on table in living room.*

2. *Place tallest roses in center, reaching out to sides.*

3. *Plan front and sides.*

4. *Fill in back with shorter stems.*

5. *Complete arrangement with ros[es] over edge of container.*

Suppose you have owned a large foliage plant—dracaena or dieffenbachia—for a year or two and it is growing so tall and thin that it is no longer a decorative addition to your living room. Only the head of the plant is beautiful now; the stem is bare and ugly. You don't want to throw it out, for it represents your first investment in a large plant.

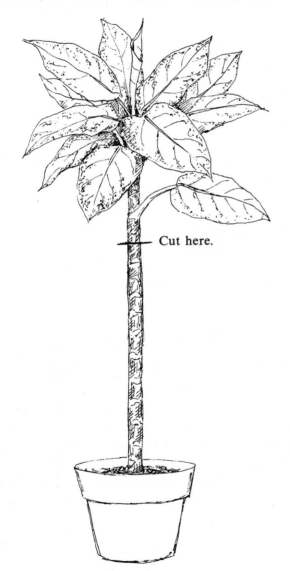

Cut here.

There is a way to save it, though it sounds drastic. Harden your heart; get out your sharpest clean knife and cut off the head of the plant. Have a large enough pot of moist

sand and peat moss waiting, dust the cut end of the plant in Hormodin #3, and put it into the rooting pot almost up to its leaves. Miracle of miracles! It will root happily in a week or two, ready for you to plant it in a new container. You are not only a propagator but you're a restorer as well! Meanwhile, trim down the thin, unattractive stem of your old plant to about 2 inches, fertilize it, and put it in a cool light spot to begin to grow again from its old roots. If you want even more dracaenas or dieffenbachias, you can cut the barren stem into pieces, each with an "eye," or growth bud, showing. Lay it lengthwise on top of the moist rooting medium, barely cover it, and wait. It will form roots that will reach down into the medium from the nodes on the stem and begin to grow up from the "eye" on the top. You'll have several little foliage plants to pot into soil and give to your friends.

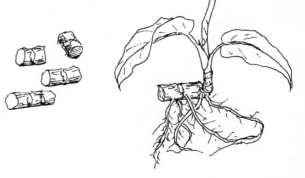

Sprinkle some Hormodin #3 onto the cut, thrust a small sterile bit of wood into the cut to keep it open, plus a little wad of moist sphagnum moss. Make a small ball of other moss, cut it in two, and bind both halves of the moss against the cut with plastic tape or plastic bags cut into wide strips so that no air can get into the wound you've

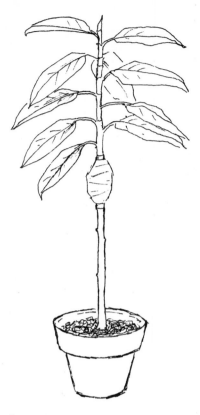

made. You can seal the edges of the plastic "bandage" with black electrician's tape or anything strong and waterproof. Now set the potted plant in a warm place but not in sun, and wait. With patience and faith, you will see roots that have formed inside the moss starting to push through it. When that happens, the new plant is ready to be disconnected from its old stem and potted handsomely in a new container.

Sowing, and the use of indoor lighting. The fourth method of supplying yourself with new plants is by starting them from seeds. Unless you have real space for this method, it is difficult to achieve with success. One way to make it not only possible but almost painless is to use fluorescent lighting. Small light units are available from special seed companies that have led the way in educating plant lovers in the use of special lights for indoor growing. You may remember references in other places in this book to the use of Gro-Lux lights to supplement natural light on potted plants near stairs or installation of fluorescent lights under a cupboard where potted herbs are

Layering. The third method of propagation is called layering. This is another way to root thick-stemmed sorts as dracaenas, rubber plants, and dieffenbachias if you prefer this method to rooting the top of the severed plant. You must have very moist sphagnum moss, which you have wet and then wrung out to keep it from being slimy. With a clean, sharp knife, cut into the stem of your plant at whatever spot you think would be appropriate for the new plant. Go almost halfway through the stem, then turn your knife and cut about 2 inches upward.

kept. In the early 1960s, people with special plant hobbies began to invest in the new fluorescent light carts on which to grow their plants. The lights were white, cool, and had the proper color spectrum to help plants grow and flower. They could be set up in a basement or an unused back hall; the lights could be turned on all day, and a collection of begonias or scented geraniums or African violets would thrive as if they were in a greenhouse. Little by little the word spread. Books were written. Experiments by lighting-fixture companies were made. New Gro-Lux 40-watt tubes, which cast a pale lavender light, were particularly good for germinating seeds and growing transplants. Seed companies such as George W. Park in South Carolina advertised a seed-starter. It came as a "table model" with a black reflector over two Gro-Lux tubes or as many as five shelves stacked one on top of another, each carrying four fluorescent bulbs, two cool white, two Gro-Lux. It was soon discovered that to maintain low-light foliage plants a special incandescent light with its red-orange-yellow lights plus a special blue to promote photosynthesis was helpful about 3 to 6 feet away from the plant. When these bulbs were close to the flat of seeds and cuttings, the heat helped hasten the germinating and rooting.

Now there's such a flood of information about using lights on growing plants in the home that you will find an embarrassment of riches from which to choose. If you want to start a few seeds in the spring, root some cuttings from special plants, begin to grow a few tuberous begonia tubers for a summer hanging basket, then treat yourself to a table-model seed-starter. With it you will receive instructions on how to use it—how far from the seeds or plants the lights should be, how many hours the lights must burn. You can purchase an automatic timer that will switch your lights on at a certain hour and turn them off when the proper time comes.

If, however, you are content to root your cuttings and start your own seeds without lights, you may want to use other special lights to illuminate the plants in your living room or family room. There are Earth Spike Grow Lamps that are fixed in a black metal spike made to be thrust into an especially lovely pot of rose geranium to bring it to bloom in the dark corner of your house where you fancy it.

There are 4-foot-long magnetic bars that hang against a wall with five openings for special incandescent lights that could be trained to any large plant you cherish. And there are small, easily clipped-on lights that can be moved wherever you need them. Look in the decorating magazines and flower catalogues to see examples of the latest lights for growing plants. Then try your own inventiveness to find a way to use these "sun substitutes" according to your own taste, for your own home.

That is one way you can show that potted plants, foliage or flowered, are worth the time and the effort you give them.

Hanging Plants:
Another Way of Bringing
Beauty Indoors

Iɴ ᴀʟʟ ʙᴜᴛ the tropical climates of Zones 9 and 10, temperatures are too cold to trust plants outside in the winter, but from Maine to Missouri, from Utah to Arkansas you can find fascinating plants hanging in bedrooms, living rooms, bathrooms, kitchens. Wherever the urge for living plants strikes the fancy, there is a place to hang a basket!

At the turn of the century the only baskets available were made of metal wire woven in plain or fancy patterns and hung in sunny windows where the trailing ivy-leaved geraniums could grow and blossom. Or they would hold a prized Boston ivy in the filtered light of the parlor where guests were entertained formally.

Today the parlor has vanished with the formality. The metal openwork wire basket in 8-inch or 12-inch diameters is still preferred by some decorators. The wire can be heavy gauge, with a dark green finish, or it can have brilliant brass finish over durable bright nickel. You can choose a molded green fiber lining or a lightweight burlap liner. You might like to try your hand at lining one yourself with old-fashioned coarse sphagnum moss or sheet moss that has been wet and squeezed out, then swirled round to fit the inside of the basket.

There are so many varieties of baskets now that you'll be hard put to choose. Plastic baskets come in pale green, decorative openwork with a liner, and also in two pieces —a pot and a matching base to catch water. You can find these in dark green, white, and clay-color. Sometimes they can be purchased in colors to match your room; otherwise you can always purchase a white one and spray it with the color you want.

You must realize, however, that the baskets won't take care of themselves. Once you have them hung—however that is going to be accomplished—they must be watered and fed. They should be taken down at least once a week for a thorough drenching in the kitchen sink. Then they will have to drain—for at least an hour—on top of a colander before you can hang them up again. The idea of watering hanging baskets with two or three ice cubes thrust on top of the soil sounds easy but doesn't seem to satisfy either the plants or their owners completely. Even the handy "snap-on" saucers underneath the new plastic pots have to be emptied if water collects in them after a thorough watering. You will have to experiment to decide whether the result is worth the effort. It must be, if you look at the pictures in the home-decorating magazines or see the lovely baskets in your florist's window. Fifty million decorators can't be wrong!

Until you have a greenhouse where water may drip without harm, you might be wise to begin your experiment with the lightest, easiest basket. That undoubtedly would be one of plastic with an attached saucer beneath it. Most basket/pots have three wires clamped to the top edge, which come together into a hook. When you have bought your pot and the plants that are to go in it, all you have to do is mix your soil. If you don't have a back yard with a good supply of rich garden soil, you can purchase a ready-made potting-soil mixture. Because your plants will need soil that will hold moisture and yet give the roots drainage, you

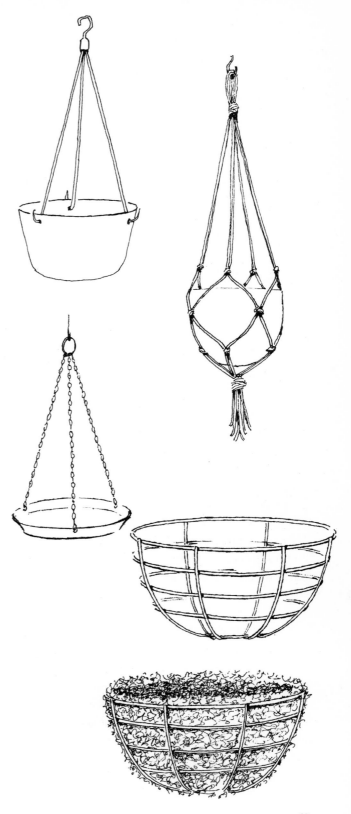

Wax Plant

your plants' needs. Just be sure to make all these decisions before you stand there waiting with the planted hanging basket in your hand!

If you live in the Northeast, Middle West, and Northwest (except for half of California, Oregon, and Washington), there are many easy plants with which to begin. The wax plant *(Hoya)* and wandering Jew *(Zebrina)* do not demand constant watering or sun. In winter the wax plant is dormant, so it is content with watering once a week. Its lovely pink blossoms come in the spring when you can fertilize the plant. The wandering Jew comes in fascinating colors: green, burgundy, lavender. It grows so fast and so well that it will soon be a charming decoration near your window.

should also purchase some peat moss and some sharp sand. Mix equal parts of soil, peat moss, and sand and fill your crocked plastic basket with it. Then carefully transplant the potted plants into their new home. If the pot is only 8 inches in diameter, three plants will do. If it is 10 or 12 inches across, you can probably put four plants around the edge and one in the center. Then water the basket/pot thoroughly, let it drain into the sink—snap on the plastic saucer—and you are ready to hang it up.

There are brackets to be screwed at the edge of the window or hooks that hang from the center of the window frame, metal poles that fit between ceiling and floor with three brackets to hold baskets, bars that can be attached to a kitchen ceiling—everything you can imagine to support a hanging basket! How you hang the basket must be your own choice, and you must choose a place to hang your basket with sufficient sun or shade for

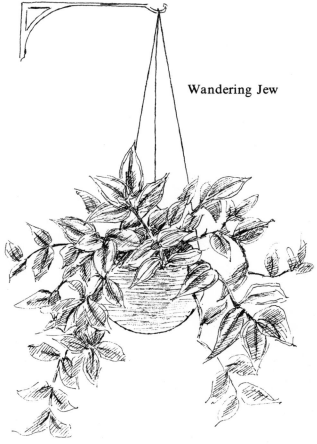

Wandering Jew

want another plant, cut the branch halfway up its length, pot the small plant in a 2-inch pot, and lo! you have a second spider plant.

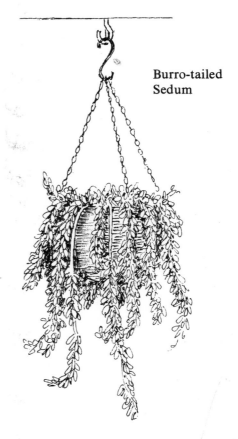

Burro-tailed Sedum

Spider Plant

Another foolproof plant to grow in a hanging basket is *Chlorophytum elatum* which you probably know well by the name of spider plant. This will live in sun or shade, have countless long branches of green and white leaves, little white flowers, and a bunch of leaves at the end of each branch. If you

A really dramatic bit of greenery is *Sedum morganiaum,* called a "burro-tailed" sedum. This is a plant you may never have known before. It is not always easy to find, but your florist can order it for you. It takes cool temperature and sunny light, and will reward you with its ease of growth and its handsome gray-green hanging foliage.

Another easy plant is kangaroo vine *(Cissus antarctica).* It will grow happily in poor light if you keep it moist, probably in a plastic pot.

A handsome unusual fern is *Pellaea rotundifolia,* known as a button fern. This has drooping leaves, looks best at eye level instead of being looked down at on a table.

It could hang from a bracket that projects from a wall, but it likes warmth and medium light.

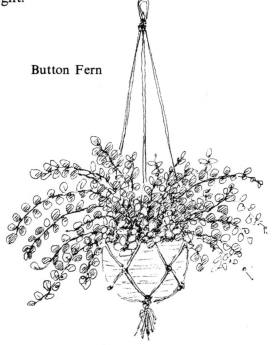

Button Fern

If you have a south or west window with lots of sunshine, then plan to hang a basket/ pot of geraniums. The ivy-leaved ones are charming or the scented ones, like rose geranium *(Pelargonium graveolens)* or the ginger or the lemon crispum *(Pelargonium crispum* group) or the nutmeg variegated *(Pelargonium fragrans)*. You can send to Howe Hill Herbs, Camden, Maine 04843, for herbs and scented geraniums if you have difficulty finding them near your home. The ivy geranium can be found at Carolbill Farm, Church Road, RD1, Brunswick, Maine 04011.

If you are interested in rare and unusual begonias, fuchsias, English ivies, cactuses, ferns, as well as in choice flowering plants, foliage, vines, and hanging basket plants, you can order them from the Merry Gardens, Camden, Maine 04843. Their catalogue is an education in itself, and the plants you order will arrive in little green plastic pots, packed as if they were jewels. Which they are.

South of the Mason-Dixon line, in Zones 6, 7, and 8, there are many beautiful blooming plants suitable for hanging baskets in addition to the ones already mentioned.

Achimenes

The tuber *Achimenes* will blossom in February in the south and bloom all spring and summer. The flowers are pink, red, orange, white, and shades of blue to purple. It likes a little sun in spring and bright shade in summer. Hang it under a tree, if you have one. Twice a month you can feed it (15–30–15) and give it lots of water. In October, when the blooms begin to fade, reduce the water until the flowers wither away. Then take down the basket/pot and put it in a dark, cool room until February, when the green will show signs of life, and you can hang it up again to start over.

Jasmine *(Jasminum gracilis magnificum)* is a lovely plant in the sunshine, putting out white fragrant blossoms.

February is the time to start trailing fuchsias—three around the edge of the basket and a matching upright one in the center. In spring and summer this beauty takes light but not full sunlight. Keep it moist and feed it every two weeks while it is growing and blooming. Many people find fish emulsion fertilizer gives excellent results. In fall it

needs to be cut back, put in a cool room to
rest through winter, then brought out in
February to sunlight again.

Lantana

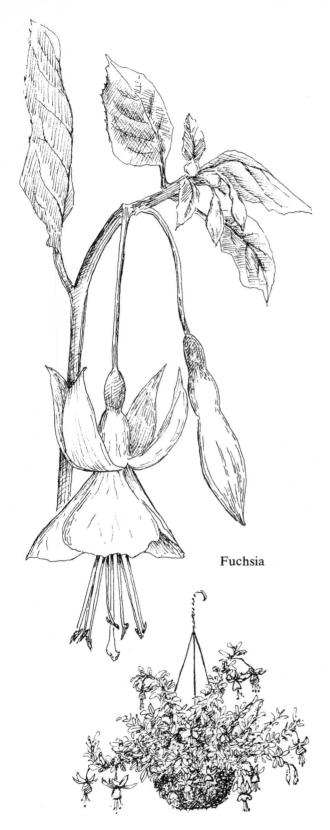

Fuchsia

Lantana *(L. montevidensis)* is trailing, with
lavender blossoms. It likes a sandy soil and
should be fertilized every other week. Give
it plenty of daylight warmth and full sun
in winter in order to have bloom. Cut it back
if necessary to keep it under control.

There's the beautiful Episcia 'Acajou' whose
foliage may be green or bronze to copper or
creamy white or pink. It is one of the loveliest hanging-basket plants. With enough
humidity and moist soil it will enjoy sun-

light in winter, but when the southern spring appears, it must be shaded or moved to a bright, not sunny, window. In the South it will bloom more reliably than in the North. When it is losing its beauty, at the end of the summer, bid it good-bye, toss it out, and buy another pot of it next February.

In South Carolina or Alabama, where spring begins by St. Valentine's Day, a hanging basket of bougainvillea would add to the beauty of any room. It should hang in the sun, where it will grow at a great pace and bloom almost constantly. 'Barbara Karst' has red flower bracts and 'Texas Dawn' is a beautiful tyrian rose. Take your pick, but be prepared to cut it off heartlessly when it seems ready to take over your room! You must keep the soil moist and feed it every two weeks. If you have a terrace or back yard where this basket can pass the summer, it would thank you for the change.

If you live in Zone 9, where the coastline brings near-tropical climates, or in Florida, which is really tropical, you can have bougainvillea growing outside on the house or as tree-shrubs. Inside, anything from orchids to petunias will grow happily as it will on a terrace or back yard. Just be sure the noon sun of winter is not too hot for the plants. You might find that ferns would provide a cooling green contrast to the hot colors outside!

One charming use of hanging baskets is a decorative one. Three, four, or five baskets can hang in a window, softening and diffusing the light in place of curtains. Ivies and ferns hanging in a bare, angular room can give a grace that would be missing otherwise. The macramé holders for baskets lend a handmade charm to a family room. There are antique wicker containers for fuchsias or begonias in a Victorian setting. Colorful Mexican woven mattings can hold a pot of "burro-tailed" sedum in a modern kitchen. All these add special decoration to your home as well as holding the greenery or flowers.

Every hanging basket becomes an expression of your personal taste and originality. That makes it especially appealing.

On pages 154–156, there is a chart of hanging plants listing the horticultural name and temperature, light, humidity, watering, and fertilizing requirements for each plant mentioned in this chapter.

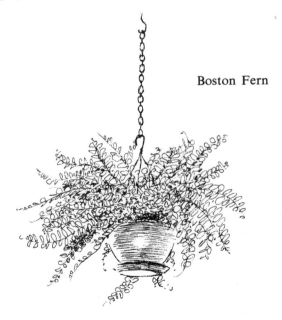

Boston Fern

Flowering Bulbs, Fragrance Plants, and Other Decorative Beauties

IF YOU COUNT as a miracle having spring bulbs bloom for you in January and February and March, when they don't appear in your outdoor garden until April, then you will have to learn the art of "forcing."

Forcing spring bulbs is one of the real adventures in decorating that you should not miss. Start experimenting with some of the bulbs suggested below. You'll never stop once you've proved to yourself that forcing is fun. It doesn't require any more effort on your part than buying some spring bulbs in the fall, as usual, some clay or plastic pots, a few labels, and some black plastic cloth. Remember how much potted hyacinths cost in February at the florist? You can purchase a dozen white hyacinth bulbs in September

for one-third that amount. The same is true of narcissuses and tulips.

Study the fall catalogues as soon as you can get them in late summer. Decide what bulbs you want to force and how many. See whether you can find pre-cooled hyacinths, which will blossom faster than ordinary ones. Study the categories of the narcissuses and tulips; a good catalogue will indicate which ones force easily. If you order your bulbs early, they will arrive, ready to be potted, from late September until mid-October.

Do you have bulb pans? These are actually shallow flowerpots, wider than they are tall. A single hyacinth bulb will need a 4-inch pot. Three bulbs of one variety will take a 6-inch pot. This same size will hold

Hyacinth

you have a yard you can put them in a cold frame, with leaves and sand piled on top to keep the bulbs from freezing and a glass cover on it when the temperature drops very low. If you don't have a yard, you can choose a corner of your garage that's not heated, or a cool room in the basement or the attic. In an apartment, put them on the lowest shelf of your refrigerator if there's no other cool place.

Once your bulbs, soil, and pots are at hand, turn your back yard, or your kitchen, into a potting shed. Scrub your old clay pots, or soak your new clay pots, or wash your new plastic pots. Cover the drainage hole or holes with broken pieces of old clay pots or round plastic drainers and a thin layer of gravel to keep the soil from draining out of the pot.

Now pour a thin layer of soil and decide how deep your bulbs must go. The tops of narcissus and hyacinth bulbs should show above the soil. Tulip bulbs should be covered by an inch of soil. When you've decided how deep the bulbs should be planted, fill the pot to that depth and set your bulbs in comfortably. Now sift the rest of the soil around and under and over the bulbs until it reaches to ½ inch below the top of the pot. Then set the pot in a shallow tray of water to soak up enough moisture to make the top soil feel damp. When the soil is completely damp, set the pot on the ground or in a kitchen colander to drain.

Write the name of the bulb on a marker, stick that at the edge of the pot, and take the bedded beauties out to whatever cool space you have chosen for them to sleep the months away. When they are settled in their cool spot (but where it won't drop below 40° F.), cover them with the black plastic to make them think they are in the ground. Look at them occasionally, and water them if the soil begins to dry out.

six tulip bulbs, five around the edge and one in the center. Three narcissus bulbs, which are large and have a "double-nosed" shape, would need a 6-inch pot, but you could get a 9-inch pot to hold five or seven narcissuses. Or you might like to use a wooden flat about 4 inches deep. You can buy either clay or plastic bulb pans. The plastic ones are lighter to carry and don't dry out as quickly as clay. They are easier to stack and don't break easily. Try both kinds, then decide which you like better.

If you have a garden, you can mix your own soil for potting: two parts garden loam; one part clean, sharp sand; one part peat moss. If you don't have a garden, there are bags of soil mix ready for you at any garden center, your florist, or a variety store.

Remember that potted bulbs, just like bulbs planted outdoors, must rest from eight to twelve weeks in a dark, cool place. If

All bulbs take a different amount of time to develop. You must check your catalogue or ask your florist which are classed as "early" or "late" forcers before you order them. Hyacinths need ten or twelve weeks in the cold, then about twenty days to bloom once they are brought into the warmth and light. You can plan to have a white 'L'Innocence' hyacinth early in January if it is pre-cooled and potted at the end of September. There are early and late blues and pinks, even a yellow. One bulb in a 4-inch pot is handsome; two single pots of the same variety are even more beautiful. You can plant three deep pink 'Jan Bos' in a 6-inch shallow pot in October to be ready for St. Valentine's Day, or plan the late white 'Carnegie' for your last hyacinth.

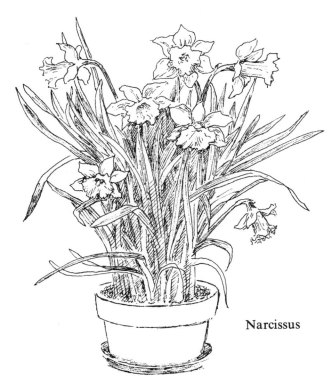

Narcissus

When you want to choose narcissuses you'll be swamped with riches. There are "trumpets," "short-cuppeds," "bi-colored" in all classes, orange, pink, white; "small-cuppeds"

called 'Jonquils'; "doubles"; "species"— your head will spin. Again, find out which come early, which late. You might want just one deep pot with five trumpets (perhaps 'Golden Harvest', early) or you might like to use one wooden flat with four rows of four different narcissuses: white trumpet 'Mount Hood', early; medium-cupped 'Duke of Windsor', medium early; Triandrus 'Thalia', medium late; Tazetta 'Geranium', late. Soon after January 1, they should be well rooted.

Take a look at one pot. Are there strong white roots showing through the bottom hole? Is the foliage showing on top? If you're not sure, you can tap the pot on its base, turn it over, and let it come out of the pot in your left hand. If the roots are strong and massed about the soil, put it back in the pot and bring it up to a warm place. Otherwise, put the pot back under the black plastic and let it wait another week, until the foliage is about 2 inches high. Don't put it into strong sunlight, but water it, let it grow, and about ten days after it has been in the warmer temperature, you will see the first trumpet budding. It takes about fourteen days for the narcissus to bloom after it has been brought from its cool bed. But that flat of different varieties of narcissuses will give you at least three weeks of bloom.

77

Tulips are even easier than narcissuses. For them you will need a 6-inch shallow bulb pan. Crock the hole, add a thin layer of gravel, then pour soil as high as you've decided you need. Put five bulbs, flat edge next to the pot, around the pot and one in the center. If you'd like red tulips for George Washington's Birthday, 'Paul Richter' is an early reliable. If you want white for Easter, 'Albino' is late and beautiful. If you get very adventuresome, you may want to try two others: the scented, early 'General de Wet' and the later lily-flowered tulip 'Jacqueline', a marvelous deep rose. That would mean you would have four pots of bulbs, at about one-half the cost of one blooming pot in March at the florist.

Tulips need twelve weeks' sleep in the cold and anywhere from fourteen to twenty-one days to bloom once they're brought into warmth. You'll learn that the closer their time is to their natural "outdoor" blooming, the less time they take to be forced. You don't have to bring all the pots out of the cold at the same time. If you do a few at a time, you will have fresh flowers from January to April.

'Paperwhite' Narcissus

Don't forget another lovely decorating bulb: 'Paperwhite' narcissus *(N. tazetta)*. These are the easiest bulbs of all—no failure, no fuss, not even soil! Because these are not always available at the local stores, you should order two or three dozen when you order your other bulbs. Order, if you need to, some pebbles or flat stones to hold the bulbs securely in the containers you select for them. Your son's glass marbles, if you can borrow them for the winter, make a perfect growing medium!

Choose your bowl: an orange one for Thanksgiving, or a small brass one, or your prized cut-glass bowl for Christmas. Fill the bowl almost to the top with the stones, pebbles, or marbles; then set the 'Paperwhites' in securely. Fill the bowl with just enough water to touch the base of the bulbs, then put it into the dark closet of the coldest

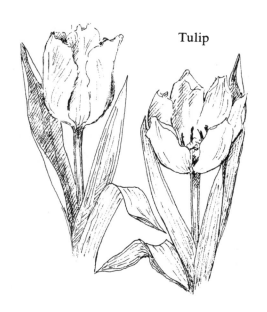

Tulip

room in your house. There it will stay until the white roots grow, fasten themselves safely around the pebbles, and the green tops reach up for the light. All you have to do is wait, adding a little water now and then as it is used by the bulbs. After about fifteen days, the roots will be strong enough to support the tall stems and flowers. Then bring the bowl out to the warmth and light of your living room or family room so everyone can enjoy the final burst of white, graceful flowers. The extra delight in these tender bulbs is their fragrance. It can fill your room with its delicate sweetness. If you start with 'Paperwhites' at different times, you can have a succession of blossoms from Thanksgiving to New Year's. When the bloom is over, the bulbs must be discarded. Wash out the bowl, rinse off the stones or pebbles, and store them for next October when you can order some more 'Paperwhites'.

These tender 'Paperwhites', like tulips, never can be forced again. If you have a garden or any small border of shrubbery, you can set the forced hyacinths and narcissuses out late in the spring when the ground is warm and frost is past. Do not cut down the foliage after the bloom is gone. Set the pot in a cool place where it will get sun or some light until it is time to plant the bulbs outside. Water it, even fertilize it, until the foliage turns yellow. This allows the strength to return to the bulbs, just as it does in the garden.

If you have space to plant outdoors, order five bulbs of *Allium giganteum* next fall. This is one of the hardy bulbs of ornamental onion. Plant them about 4 inches deep at the back of your border and watch them grow 4 feet tall in June or July. Cut two of them when the blossoms are starry blue and round as a grapefruit, condition them for an hour in deep water, then arrange them in a bronze, footed bowl. Let the taller one soar about 3 feet into the air, with the second one,

cut to about 2 feet, placed directly below. At the base, put three heart-shaped wild-ginger leaves, each one's stem about 2 inches longer than the other and encircling the stem of the one above, with all three encircling the stems of the *Allium*. It will be a traffic stopper in your entrance hall!

You will enjoy their beauty for at least ten days. Then, as the color fades, take the arrangement away, but hang the two *Allium* (carefully, head down, so one doesn't touch the other), until they dry to a wonderful sandy beige shade. Then they will be ready for your fall and winter arrangements. Turn to page 64a to see how striking they can be.

But don't give all your secrets away. There's one you might keep for your own special delight. This is the pineapple lily *(Eucomis)*. If

Pineapple Lily

you've never seen this plant, ask your florist to order it for you. It is available at most specialty growers. You will have to pot this bulb yourself, according to the directions the grower will supply. It takes at least a 7-inch pot, preferably an 8- to 10-inch one, for the roots are extensive and the leaves are large and handsome. Place it where it will get direct light, and water it sparingly. It takes from sixty to seventy-five days to bloom, but the tall white flower stalk will last two months or more. Treat yourself and your home to this unusual plant. It is not expensive and it will last many seasons.

Fragrance Plants and Other Beauties

Flowering plants are always a decorator's joy, and those that are fragrant offer a very special added pleasure.

Do you know *Osmanthus fragrans?* Its other name is sweet olive. It might become your favorite indoor shrub; dark green, tough leaves with small white very fragrant flowers that bloom year round. It would be charming on your family-room table.

Sweet Olive

There's Madagascar jasmine *(Stephanotis floribunda)* with leathery leaves, twining

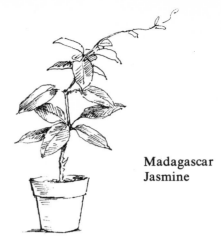

Madagascar Jasmine

stems. If it's not available at your florist, you can order a small pot of it from a specialty greenhouse. Start it in your sunniest room with a little trellis to climb. Its fragrant waxy white flowers smell like a wedding!

Dwarf Orange

Long-lasting *Citrus cadmonium* is a dwarf orange that bears numerous small fruit on a slender tree. Another heavenly smelling vine, poet's jasmine *(Jasminum officinale grandiflorum)* is a shrubby vine with fragrant white starlike flowers that bloom over a long period. You can't have every room in your house decked out for a wedding, but one of these would add green and flower and fragrance to any room.

There are other plants whose blooms are fascinating and whose life is hardy. The

Abutilon hybrid called flowering maple has showy bell-like flowers in apricot, pink, white, red. It blooms continuously. The strange bird-of-paradise *(Strelitzia)* with its exotic orange and blue blooms is always tempting. It grows fast, but you might have to wait five years for it to blossom! Not so the shrimp plant *(Beloperone guttata),* a name you will understand as soon as you see the color and shape of its blossom. It blooms constantly, will go outside happily in the summer and supply you with rooted cuttings whenever you wish to increase your stock.

If you have a window with light but no sun, pots of impatiens hybrids, the low variety, will bloom happily all winter, as will the begonia in a sunny window—almost any one of its hundreds of varieties.

If you live in a tropical climate such as Florida or Southern California, where frost comes rarely, you have the right weather for growing geranium "trees." Otherwise you must grow them after frost in spring and take them indoors when frost threatens in fall. But no matter where you live, geranium trees could be handsome guardians of your front stoop, if you live in a small city house, or they would be most attractive on a sunny terrace or in a back yard. These trees are simple to create. All you have to do is harden your heart to all the shoots and twigs along the stem of the potted geranium; pull off all the leaves and branches, as it struggles upward; then, when it is as tall as you wish, pinch all its topmost branches so that the foliage will grow, and it will bloom in glory!

Another handsome tree can be made from a hibiscus shrub. This is also a tropical plant that cannot live outdoors where frost could nip it. But inside your apartment or house, potted in a large tub of plastic or imitation-Italian pottery, it will grow happily in the sunshine of your family room or sunporch. It will provide you with double flowers of red, pink, coral, or white most of the year. It is not a fussy plant. It will grow outdoors during the summer with little effort on your part. On page 96d you can see how decorative a hibiscus tree can be without a single blossom. The fresh green foliage alone is charming.

All you have to do is decide which of these plants would bring you pleasure and solve your decorating needs best, then try one. The chart on pages 142–152 lists the temperature, light, humidity, watering, and feeding requirements for each of the plants mentioned here.

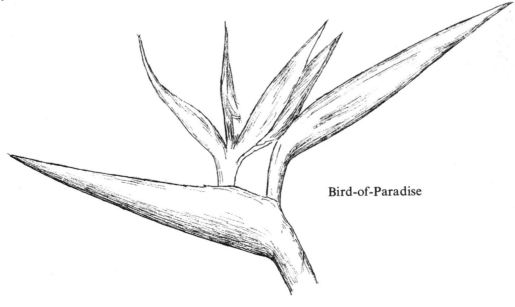

Bird-of-Paradise

Preserving
Fresh Flowers and Greens

SOMETIMES, as you are dismantling a flower arrangement, you are tempted to save an appealing pale marigold or a tall blue salvia. The foliage is gone, but the flower blossom is still lovely, even though it is dry. What would happen if you just left it in its container? Would it last? Would it die? The blue salvia would dry perfectly if you took off its leaves and hung it, head down, in a warm, dry room. The marigold cannot be dried quite as easily. It belongs to the group of flowers that require a special drying agent (which we will discuss later).

Some flowers actually last "forever" with no help at all. The Greeks had a word, *amaranth,* which means "everlasting," "not withering." When you see that in the name of a flower, you know it is one of the immortals.

About fifteen such plants (described on pages 83–85), are still available today.

If you have a garden you might want to plant coxcomb *(Celosia)* or strawflowers

(Helichrysum bracteatum) and enjoy their fresh color and beauty all summer, then cut them and put them in an arrangement without water for the fall and winter. These and the others listed can be found easily at your florist or garden shop all through the fall.

Then there are the flowers and shrubs and trees and vines (described on pages 86 and 87) which dry naturally and easily.

The method of preserving these flowers is simple. Take off the leaves. If the blossoms are not too large, dry them in bundles. Tie a bunch together gently near their heads and at the end of their stems. Then hang them, head down, in a dark room or closet—the attic, the garage, an unused closet. If the blossoms are large, be sure that they don't touch each other. You can hang them from a high rope or rod or even from wire coat hangers in a closet. Give them about two weeks to dry out completely. Then use them at once, if you need them, or store them upright or in a box for use later in the year.

82

Everlasting Flowers

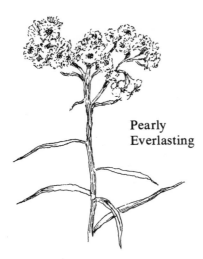

Pearly
Everlasting

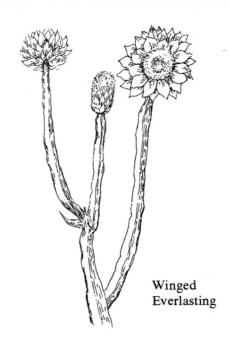

Winged
Everlasting

Pearly Everlasting
(Anaphalis margaritacea)
Pearl-white. Weedy perennial. 18–30 inches.

Swan River Everlasting
(Helipterum manglesii)
White or pink daisy-like flower with yellow
center. Annual. 8–15 inches.

Winged Everlasting
(Ammobium alatum grandiflorum)
White, woolly leaves and yellow heads.
Perennial. 1–3 feet.

Strawflower

Love-Lies-Bleeding

Strawflower
(Helichrysum bracteatum)
Yellow, orange, red, pink or white.
Annual. 12–30 inches.

Love-Lies-Bleeding
(Amaranthus caudatus)
Red. Annual. 12–30 inches.

Coxcomb
(Celosia argentea cristata)
Prevailing red, but also comes in apricot, gold, silver. Grows in strange cluster like a giant rooster's comb. Annual. 8 inches–2½ feet.

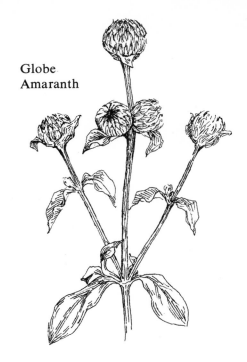

Globe
Amaranth

Globe Amaranth
(Gomphrena globosa)
Red, pink, white and orange. Annual. 12–20 inches.

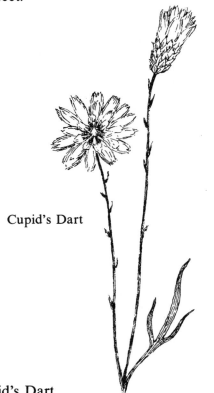

Cupid's Dart

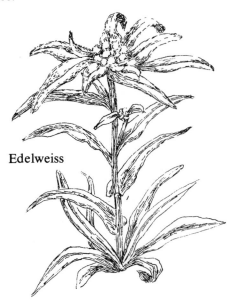

Edelweiss

Cupid's Dart
(Catananche caerulea)
Blue (the only blue perennial everlasting). 12–18 inches.

Edelweiss
(Leontopodium alpinum)
White flower with woolly bracts; Alpine perennial. 5–7 inches.

Immortelle
(Xeranthemum annuum)
Pink, purple, rose, red, and white. Annual
2–3 feet.

Summer Cypress or
Burning Bush
(Kochia scoparia trichophila)
Bright green, turning, in fall, to brilliant
crimson. Handsome foliage.
Annual. 30 inches.

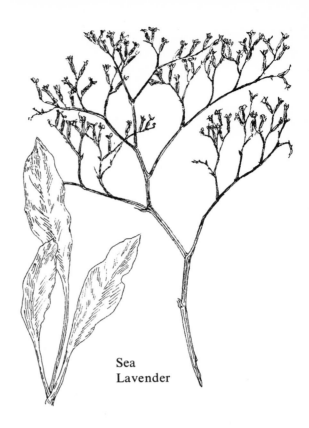

Sea
Lavender

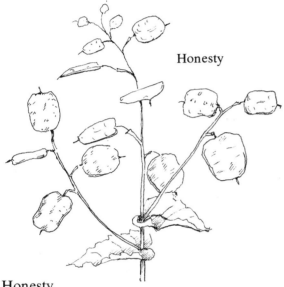

Honesty

Honesty
(Lunaria annua)
Round, silvery pods. Biennial. 18–30 inches.

Sea Lavender
(Limonium latifolium)
Branching cloudlike clusters of tiny flowers.
Perennial. 15–24 inches.

Prickly
Thrift

Thrift

Prickly Thrift
(Acantholimon glumaceum)
Rose-pink, fragrant flower. Evergreen
leaves. Perennial. 4–6 inches.

Thrift
(Armeria maritima)
Purple and white. Fine rock garden plant.
Perennial. 6–12 inches.

Flowers, Shrubs and Trees that Dry Naturally

FLOWERS

Ornamental onion, bulb
(Allium giganteum)
Deep blue, round blossoms. Plant in fall.

Ornamental
Onion

Baby's Breath

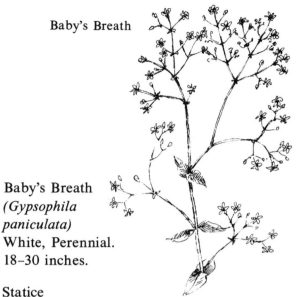

Baby's Breath
*(Gypsophila
paniculata)*
White, Perennial.
18–30 inches.

Statice
(Limonium sinuatum)
All colors including white. Delicate, airy.
Perennial in south. Annual in north.
12 inches–1½ feet.

Summer Salvia
(Salvia farinacea)
Blue, tall. Annual in north.
Perennial in south. 3 feet.

SHRUBS

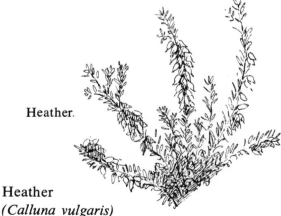

Heather.

Heather
(Calluna vulgaris)
An evergreen sub-shrub. Flowers include
purple, white, red, pink. 8–15 inches.

Scotch Broom

Scotch Broom
(Cytisus scoparius)
Wonderful green stems. 4–9 feet.

Heath
(Erica)
Evergreen European shrub. Flowers scarlet, pink, red, white. 8–12 inches.

Hydrangea

Hydrangea
(Hydrangea macrophylla)
Huge heads of blooms. Can be left on shrub till almost dry, then cut. 3–4 feet.

TREES

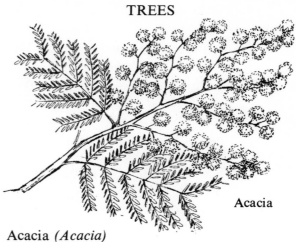

Acacia

Acacia *(Acacia)*
Beautiful golden ball blossoms in sprays with feathery leaves. 15 feet.

Silver Dollar Tree
(Eucalyptus cinerea)
Round leaves along the stem; will dry silver. 30 feet.

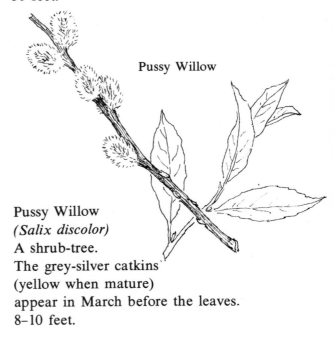

Pussy Willow

Pussy Willow
(Salix discolor)
A shrub-tree.
The grey-silver catkins
(yellow when mature)
appear in March before the leaves.
8–10 feet.

VINE

Bittersweet
(Celastrus scandens)
Yellow berries with flaming burnt orange color beneath. 20–40 feet.

87

Some flowers require the application of a drying compound to retain their natural beauty. For many years, sand or a combination of borax and oatmeal was sifted over the flowers to dry and preserve them. Now there is a material called silica gel that is easier to use and is more effective. It can be bought in one-pound and five-pound cans. It looks and feels like salt or sugar, can be used again and again, and works quickly and successfully.

There is another product very much like it, called Flower-Dri, which has the added feature of a bright blue color that changes to indicate the amount of moisture it has absorbed. After two or three uses, the blue fades to a pale pink, indicating that it has absorbed moisture. When you see the change of color, you know the Flower-Dri has done its job and needs to be dried out before it can be used again. To dry it out, pour the Flower-Dri into a shallow pan; set it in an oven at 275°–300° for about 20 minutes. When the blue color returns, take the Flower-Dri out, pour it back into its original can, cover it, and let it cool. Then it is ready to be used again.

Drying flowers that require a drying compound takes patience and a little easily acquired skill. Have the silica gel or the Flower-Dri ready on the counter or table you are going to use, along with a spool of florist's wire #23, garden clippers that can cut wire, and lots of newspaper to catch any mess. And, of course, the flowers you are going to dry. This is not a complicated task if you begin with some simple flowers, say, five small zinnias and three shasta daisies.

If you grow the flowers in your own sunny border, cut them at about ten or eleven o'clock in the morning, when all the dew and moisture have evaporated. If you buy them at your florist or roadside stand, take them home and process them as quickly as possible. In both cases, make sure you have chosen flowers that are at the height of their beauty. No matter how successfully you dry them, you cannot make flowers any more perfect in color or texture than they are when you begin.

Look among your "treasures" for a metal can or a large cookie box with a tight-fitting lid. If you do not have a metal can or box, you can use a tough cardboard box. Just be sure to make the corners moisture-proof by sealing them with mailing tape on the outside.

First cut off the stem of the flower to about ¾ of an inch below the blossom. Then cut a piece of wire about 3 or 4 inches long and run the end of it into the short stem and into the base of each daisy. Don't let the wire show in the face of the flower. Zinnias have a hollow stem, so you may push your wire all the way through the blossom, curve it down about ½ inch along itself, and gently pull the wire until it hooks into the zinnia center.

Now pour about ¾ of an inch of the Flower-Dri into the metal can or cardboard box. With this mattress of Flower-Dri in the can or box, you are now ready to put your flowers "to bed." Many people prefer to put the blossoms facedown. Some prefer to bend the wire stem at an angle so the flowers can be faceup. Try both methods to see which makes the flowers look most natural. No matter how you place the flowers, you must pour the Flower-Dri gently along the edges of the can or box until it makes its way under and over the petals of the flower. You'll soon see why a flat-petaled zinnia is easier to dry than the shaggy-petaled variety. Make sure all the spaces are filled with the Flower-Dri. Tap the top or side of the can or box to make sure there are no open spaces, then gently cover the top (or the base) of the blossoms by sifting

more Flower-Dri over them through a small strainer. Put on the top of the can or box, mark it with the date, the name of the flower, and the date when it will be ready. Then put the can on a top shelf, where it won't be disturbed. These flowers should be ready for you to take out in three days.

When that great day arrives, put the handy old newspapers on your counter again, plus the container for the Flower-Dri. Take off the cover of the can or box. If the flowers are facedown, hold the wire stems firmly in your left hand while you pour the drying material from the drying box back into its own container. If the flowers are faceup, pour *very* carefully so as not to hurt the dried blossoms. Remove the flowers and brush off any remaining grains of Flower-Dri with a soft, dry paint brush before you really draw a breath to see the results.

There you will behold three beautiful white shasta daisies and five glowing pink zinnias, ready to be put into an everlasting arrangement.

On pages 90 and 91 there are pictures of some of the flowers you can dry with Flower-Dri, plus the time each needs to become dry. There are many more, but you will be wise to start with these familiar, fairly easy-to-dry flowers, doing a few at a time until you feel experienced enough to tackle others.

After you have had some experience drying flowers, you will probably devise some special methods of your own. In the meantime, here are some hints that may be helpful.

• Cup-shaped flowers, like roses and platycodons, will need to be cushioned on a little "hill" of Flower-Dri so that you can slide the drying material underneath the blossom as well as between the petals.

• Marigolds have a heavy base. You can run the wire through the base about ½ inch, then bend it back and twist it around the rest of the wire.

• Snapdragons and delphiniums will be easier to arrange if you dry them on their stalks. This will mean using a long florist's box and maybe a supporting cardboard or two beneath the stems to make it easier to get the Flower-Dri underneath them. You don't have to cover the box of stalks. Just put it in a warm, dark room or closet for the necessary drying period.

Year-round shrubs and trees furnish foliage and leaves that are stunning with fresh spring and summer flowers. And even your dried flowers need greens when you use them in arrangements in fall and winter. The greens are so simple to preserve in glycerine (see pages 92–94), so available from your own garden or from your florist, that you can preserve some almost every month of the year. Just store them in boxes or dry bottles until you need them.

Flowers that Can Be Dried with Flower-Dri

ANNUALS

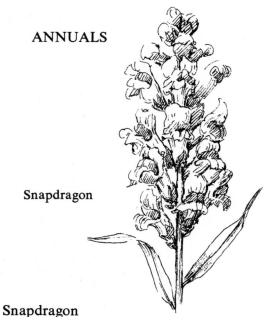

Snapdragon

Snapdragon
(Antirrhinum)
Use open-blossom variety 'Bright Butterfly' or 'Little Darling'. Time needed: flower, 3 days; stalk, 5 days.

Dahlia
Time needed: 4 days.

Marigold

Marigold
(Tagetes)
Time needed: small flower, 4 days; large flower, 7 days.

Zinnia
(Zinnea elegans)
Use flat-petalled blossoms. Don't use red; color unsatisfactory. Time needed: 3 days.

BIENNIALS

Queen Anne's Lace
(Daucus carota)
Tough stem, don't cut off. Dry face-down. Time needed: 4 days.

Sunflower

Sunflower
(Helianthus annuus)
Time needed: 4 days.

Queen Anne's Lace

Pansy

Pansy
(Viola tricolor hortensis)
Time needed: 5 days.

PERENNIALS

Shasta Daisy

Shasta Daisy
(Chrysanthemum maximum)
Time needed: 3 days.

Chrysanthemum *(C. morifolium)*
Don't use red or orange. Color not good.
Time needed: button mums, 4 days; large
flowers, 7 days.

Delphinium *(D. hybridum)*
Time needed: single flower, 3 days; stalk,
5 days.

Balloon Flower

Balloon Flower
(Platycodon grandiflorum)
Not necessary to wire. Time needed: 4 days.

SHRUBS

Geranium
(Pelargonium hybrids)
Cut stem 1 inch below cluster. Time
needed: 4 days.

Rose
(Rosa)
Not dark red. Color unsatisfactory. Time
needed: 5 days.

Foliage that Can Be Preserved with Glycerine

SHRUBS

Boxwood
(Buxus sempervirens suffruticosa)
Time needed: 3–4 days. Color changes to green.

Mountain Laurel

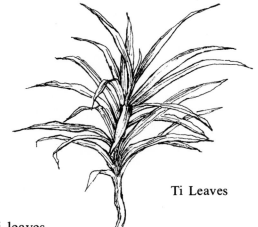

Ti Leaves

Ti leaves
(Cordyline terminalis)
Time needed: 2 days.

Mountain Laurel
(Kalmia latifolia)
Foliage only. Time needed: 4 days. Color changes to bronzy-green.

Juniper *(Juniper communis depressa)*
Foliage only. Time needed: 4 days.

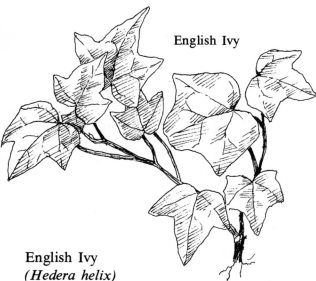

English Ivy

Azalea

English Ivy
(Hedera helix)
Put leaves and stems in solution. Time needed: 2 days.

Iris *(Iris bearded hybrids)*
Foliage only. Time needed: 2 days.

Azalea, evergreen
(Rhododendron Kurume hybrids)
Foliage only. Time needed: 3 days. Color changes to olive green.

Rhododendron *(R. maximum)*
Foliage only. Time needed: 4 days. Color changes to bronzy-green.

92

TREES

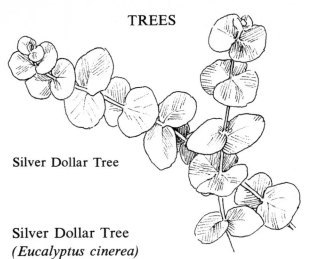

Silver Dollar Tree

Silver Dollar Tree
(Eucalyptus cinerea)
Time needed: 3 days. Color changes to
mahogany red or silver green.

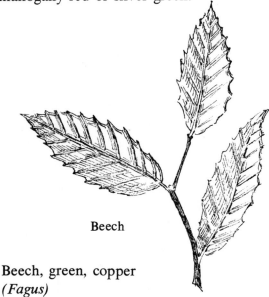

Beech

Beech, green, copper
(Fagus)
Time needed: 4 days. Color changes to
green, darkening to brown.

American Holly
(Ilex opaca)
Time needed: 4 days. Color changes to
olive green.

Bull Bay
(Magnolia grandiflora)
Time needed: 3 weeks. Color changes to
beautiful brown.

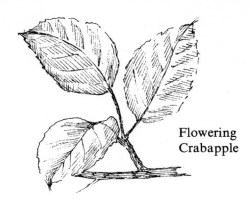

Flowering
Crabapple

Flowering Crabapple
(Malus floribunda)
Time needed: 4 days. Color changes to
bronzy green.

Purple-leaf Plum
*(Prunus cerasifera
var. pissardii)*
Time needed: 3 days. Color changes to
deep purple.

Pear
(Pyrus communis)
Time needed: 3 days, color changes to
bronze; 4 days, color changes to brown.

Pin Oak
(Quercus palustris)
Time needed: 4 days. Color changes to
autumn tones in fall.

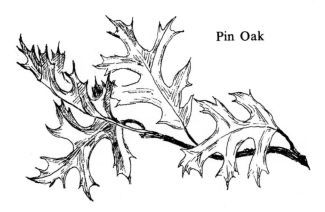

Pin Oak

All you need to preserve greens is glycerine (which you can buy at your drugstore), water, and a tall, narrow jar. A 1-quart Mason jar is adequate to hold six or eight sprays of most leaves. Make sure, of course, that the jar will not tip over with the foliage in it. Either support it on each side with heavy bookends or by putting a heavy metal flower holder in the bottom of the jar. Mix one part glycerine with two parts warm water. You will need about 6 inches of the liquid in the jar. Stir it thoroughly. Now you're ready for your foliage.

What shall it be? Again, there are many leaves that you could try. On pages 92 and 93 you will find some of the most attractive for use in arrangements, with special instructions where needed, and the number of days each will need in the glycerine solution. Changes in color are noted in cases where they occur.

With the glycerine and water mixture ready, wipe off any dust or dirt on the foliage, peel up the bark 4 or 5 inches from the end of the shrub or branch, and hammer it until it is frayed and ready to absorb the solution. Stand it immediately in the glycerine solution and place it where it can rest safely for the requisite time. Be sure you have a tall enough, strong enough container for the magnolia branches. These are so prized by their owners in the South, where they grow, and so difficult to purchase from greenhouses in the North, that they are worthy of any effort involved in preserving them. You can watch the color change from green to pale tan, then to a deep chocolate brown so that you can almost tell when the glycerine solution has been completely absorbed. Once saturated, the leaves will last almost forever. They can be your "jewel" decoration, no matter where you place them. They can be combined with live flowers, without being hurt by the water. Even the individual leaves serve as a rich background for the glowing colors of fresh blossoms.

Don't forget there are wild flowers, herbs, and grasses that are yours for the picking and easy to dry. All they need is a tall vase to hold them. There are cattails in marshy spots, both small and large, waiting for you to cut them in June or before July 4. They'll dry a light tan and be your favorite in fall arrangements with colorful gourds and fall squash. In midsummer you'll find black-eyed susans, yarrow, and wheat. In September the wild asters and, in your own herb garden, fragrant lavenders, tall red *Monarda*, and the lovely round blue blossoms of chives.

Of course, you can't spend all your time preserving flowers and greens! But, year round, you can keep your eyes open for possible materials that you will want to use in arrangements to decorate your home. Once these materials are preserved, you can use what you need at that moment and pack the rest in a box or put them in a sturdy vase to wait until you need them again. No matter how beautiful they are, you don't want more than one dried arrangement in a room.

When the time comes to change to fresh flowers, there's an easy way to store your dried arrangement. Fasten a piece of dry styrofoam to a large needle flower holder and place it in an open bowl. Insert the dried flowers in the styrofoam and put the bowl on an unused shelf—preferably in a closet where the flowers will collect a minimum of dust.

The pleasure you will gain from learning these simple methods of keeping spring and summer flowers "alive and well" in fall and winter will increase as your skill increases. The colors, forms, and lines of your decorating year will not fade completely. You will be able to store some of the beauty in a corner of your house as well as in your memory.

Decorating for All Seasons

No MATTER where you live, January is the first month to bring out your earliest forced bulbs, probably the pre-cooled hyacinth 'L'Innocence'. It will take about twenty days for it to bloom after you bring it up, twelve days in cool light and eight in warm light. It will look to you the loveliest white flower that you have ever made possible! It will be as much at home in the kitchen, next to the little potted herbs, as it will in your living room (see page 96d).

By February the earliest narcissuses are rooted enough for you to bring them out of the cold; they will require about fourteen days to bloom. The early tulips require from fourteen to twenty-one days. With luck, you should have red ones ready for George Washington's Birthday.

In February, don't forget to buy at least three begonia tubers to start for summer bloom outside. Decide whether you want the American double-ruffled hybrids, called 'Ballerina Strain', the 'Double Rose Form', or the 'Picotee', which is also double ruffled but has the edge marked in a different color. They all come in marvelous shades: yellow, red, scarlet, salmon, pink, and white. Get the fattest, healthiest tubers you can find at the garden shop or florist or from a specialty begonia grower. Purchase a bag of milled sphagnum moss; pour that into a shallow plastic flat, then press the begonia tubers into it firmly. Be sure you have the flat, cuplike side of the tuber on the top, then mist the sphagnum moss thoroughly. If you have a Gro-Lux table-model seed-starter, put your begonias under the lights and set them for whatever time your direction booklet advises. The roots will grow down, leaves will appear on the top, and you will soon be able to pot each plant into a 5-inch pot. Keep them warm, out of sunlight, and with plenty of moisture. By May, when the danger of frost is gone, you can set them in the shade of your border to bloom all summer, still in their pot.

March is spring in half of these United States, but it still can be winter in the other half. If you become impatient waiting for spring to arrive, you might consider pruning a few branches from your shrubs or trees and bringing them indoors to unfold their blossoms or leaves. No matter what part of the country you live in, you can find a day in January, February, or March when the temperature has risen enough so that the branches are not frozen. Choose a time around midday. With a slightly slanting angle, cut several long branches with lots of buds on them. Inside your house, trim off any dead wood, then hammer the stems an inch or two from the end and put them into a tall pail of warm water. Let them stay at room temperature, but not in direct sunlight, until you see the charming blossoms or leaves unfold. The closer to their natural time of blooming you cut them, the shorter

time it will take for them to open. Shrubs whose blossoms come out before their leaves are fastest to force. Here are a few of the welcome signs of spring you might like to try:

	TIME TO CUT	FORCING TIME
Barberry, green or red	mid-March	2 weeks
Flowering crabapple	early March	2–4 weeks
Flowering dogwood	mid-March	2 weeks
Forsythia	early Feb.	2 weeks
	early March	10 days
	late March	1 week
Japanese maple tree	early March	2 weeks
Red maple tree	mid-March	1 week
Tulip tree (South Carolina)	late Feb.	3 weeks
Pussy willow (cultivated)	Feb.	1–2 weeks

When you have pussy willows that you have forced, or if you purchase them later, always use at least twelve or sixteen twigs at once, sometimes of different heights. They will look more graceful in an arrangement if they are curved rather than straight. Manipulate the stems in your fingers after they have soaked up enough water to be pliable. Take four or five of them at one time, hold them in your hands in a horizontal position with your two thumbs positioned under the stems. Then gently, forcefully, bend them in the direction you want them to be—in one curve or two. They will not break if you aren't rough with them, but will gradually assume a lovely curve. When you are satisfied with their shape, then arrange them on a flower holder to set the scene for whatever other flowers you will combine in the arrangement: narcissuses, tulips, pansies, crabapple blossoms, grape hyacinths, or primroses. Anything that means spring to you.

If you decide to use the pussy willows by themselves, it is not necessary to keep them in water. If they are in water too long, they will develop catkins, which are not very attractive.

Flowering Crabapple

Ideas for Winter

*When snow and ice decorate the out-of-doors, flowers and plants
are doubly welcome for indoor decorating. A quiet cup of tea is
enhanced by colorful miniature and dwarf geraniums placed on
a gravel base in a copper tray. Plastic pots painted to blend with
the woodwork. Collection: 'Skies of Italy', 'Poinsettia', 'Gibbosum',
'Dasycaulon', 'Echinatum', 'Fair Ellen', 'Doc', 'Tammy', 'Pixie'.
Dried German statice fills a Staffordshire finger vase.*

New Year's Day Open House Reception. Lace cloth. Silver bowl and cups of eggnog in foreground. At far end, silver urn for coffee service. Arrangement of flowers in footed silver bowl: snapdragons, carnations, stock, roses.
Green candles in silver candlesticks. Traditional cookies in antique German forms: high-hatted men, women, stars, rocking horses, all hand-decorated.

96b

LEFT: *How to decorate with space! Healthy, flourishing potted greens and trees in handsome containers are sustained by four long Gro-Lux bulbs fastened to the overhead base of the stair landing. June in January!*

BELOW: *Charming Christmas decorations center on Scotch pine tree hung with red silk balls on outside balcony. Indoors, year-round avocado "tree" ceiling-high, cool green* Dieffenbachia Zebra, *schefflera, and a blooming white camelia 'C. H. Wilson'. On the far table, red azaleas. Foreground, poinsettia.*

ABOVE: *Sun porch in February, gay with potted plants. Large hibiscus tree on green iron stand. On low black table is a dragon tree, grown from seed from Canary Islands. On floor, two pots of red 'Paul Richter' tulips, forced in October. Behind other chair, two pale pink 'Carefree' geranium trees, raised from seed. On tile table, a pink and white Belgian amaryllis.*

RIGHT: *Even in winter, herbs are a herald of spring! Collection in green plastic pots: Lemon Crispum fingerbowl geranium, chives, rosemary, English thyme, sorrel, lavender, marjoram, bay, tarragon. In sunny corner of counter, blooming white hyacinth 'L'Innocence', forced in autumn, and green pot of parsley.*

96d

A charming picture can be made by using the pussy willows and flowers in a black cup pin holder on a shallow, dull green tray, with the arrangement set at one end of the shallow water and the cup hidden by small yew *(Taxus)* clippings and irregular Japanese stones, black and gray, leading from the base to the right under the water.

If you have not discovered the beauty of the potted plant Kafir lily *(Clivia miniata),* March might be a good time to get acquainted. Your florist might not have one for you to see, but you might be able to see it at a public conservatory or at least in a book at the library. It is a member of the amaryllid family—has evergreen straplike foliage and is beautiful in a sunless, bright warm room. When it blooms—or *if* it blooms —it has a radiantly orange cluster of lilies that lasts for weeks. But *Clivia* has a need for resting at least three or four months when it doesn't even need water. Then, in March or April, you can give it not only water but a little fertilizer and you will see the green stalk rising, which will become its blossom. It is not an inexpensive plant. Make sure you want it before you order it from your florist. Then, when it blooms, you will be delighted that you gave yourself a spring present.

Kafir Lily

Spring itself will bring you some gifts. In Vermont, near icy streams, there'll be marsh marigolds *(Caltha palustris),* waiting to be gathered and arranged in a low tin-lined straw basket with blue forget-me-nots *(Myosotis alpestris).*

In Kentucky the white dogwood tree *(Cornus florida)* is blooming. In Minnesota the forsythia and bridal wreath *(Spiraea vanhouttei)* are jeweling the May countryside, while in Ohio the peonies are in full bloom, with the lilacs *(Syringa)* almost ready to burst open in Chicago. In South Carolina and Georgia it is already hot weather by Memorial Day, while in Wisconsin the late tulips are tall and perfect. This rich and lovely land offers all its perfumed treasure of bulbs and shrubs to all its people. Make sure you bring some of this spring fragrance into your home. Find containers to hold these flowering shrubs that are worthy of them: a tall black vase with a simple line of great beauty to hold the dogwood branch in your entrance hall. It echoes the black mark on the white petal of the blossom and satisfies you each time you look at it. As for the peonies, just two double red blossoms—one budding, the other in full bloom—rising up from a glass footed bowl, with one leaf hanging over the rim to accent the arrangement, will fill your living room with perfume.

97

If you have a terrace, a porch, or a back yard, then the trailing fuchsia (in shade) or the luscious hanging tuberous begonia (also in shade) will be worth your effort. In bright sunlight the 'Cascade' petunia (white, pink, coral, red) and the ivy-leaf geranium as well as the smaller-growing regular geranium are beautiful all summer long. Do try the *Browallia speciosa major,* which may be unknown to you but which is a marvelous shade of blue and will bloom all summer long, in sun or with only half a day of sun. It comes also in white, but is not as spectacular. Another lovely annual is *Lobelia gracilis,* which is blue and trailing.

'Cascade' Petunia

When summer finally comes there is sometimes a special occasion for which to decorate your home with fresh flowers: a wedding! Nothing is more suitable to honor a bride than lilies. In Zones 4, 5, and 6, lilies begin to bloom in late May with the early Asiatic hybrids: some flowers upright, some outward-facing, and some pendant. In June and July the Aurelian hybrids—trumpets, bowl-shaped, or sunburst types—

can turn your garden, even with only three bulbs blooming, into a paradise of fragrance. Into August and September the Oriental hybrids—bowl-shaped flowers, flat-faced, or recurved flowers—present a breathtaking beauty unequaled by any other blooms. Many of them are the result of years of inspired experiments by horticulturists all over America, among whom Jan de Graaff, formerly owner of the Oregon Bulb Farms in Gresham, Oregon, stands out as a champion. A charming man, he is responsible for the present classification of lily bulbs into their reasonable order and developing some of the most stunning hardy hybrids. His nonstop journeys over the United States, Canada, England, and Holland breathed life into lily societies from state to international groups. His humor made a lifelong convert of one woman who had ordered three bulbs of 'Empress of India' about which she had just read in a garden section of the *New York Times.* De Graaff wrote to confirm her letter but added, "I have taken the liberty of substituting another bulb for the 'Empress of India'. This is their first season on sale and they cost, wholesale, fifty dollars each!"

You will not have to invest very much to plant the 'Empress' today. If you are able to have a partially shaded area to grow a few lilies, you might like three 'Corsage', a salmon-pink outward-facing Asiatic (dainty, multiflowered early bloomer); and six 'Enchantment', a nasturium red upright-flowered lily that is so unbeatable it is patented. Behind these you could plant three trumpet lilies, 'Green Magic', plus 'Jamboree', an Oriental hybrid that rises 5 or 6 feet tall with white recurved flowers dotted with crimson markings. There's no way to describe the beauty of the different varieties. The elegant 'Imperial' Oriental hybrids come in crimson, gold, pink, and silver. They are

Lily

flat-faced flowers; each opens widely, has stripes of color dividing each petal, and markings of its color on them. If you live where winters are severe, it is wise to plant these Oriental hybrids in the spring. Order them the fall before; tell the lily supplier what planting date you want and have everything ready when the bulbs arrive. It is wise to plant the species lily—*Lilium martagon album* or *L. martagon* 'Pink'—in the spring, also. The other lilies can be safely planted in the fall.

Lilium martagon album is a beautiful white lily whose petals curl back upon themselves showing only the gold stamens as color. One full blossom, arranged by yourself or your florist, as a corsage, is more elegant for the mother of the bride or groom to wear to a wedding than an orchid, and about one-third the price. If you find a catalogue of the varieties of lilies—perhaps

the colored list from Oregon Bulb Farms, P.O. Box 529, Gresham, Oregon 87030— and decide what lilies you would like to order to decorate your home for a wedding reception or dinner, your florist will be able to order them in bloom for you. They can be sent to you by airmail or by Greyhound bus. They will arrive packed in tight, unopened bud, anywhere from seven to sixteen blooms to each stalk. Take them out of the box; put them in deep, cool water. They will begin to open in an hour. Pinch out the stamens in each blossom. Handsome as they are in the garden, they will stain a dress or furniture cover if they touch it. They will also stain the lily's petals! If you can find peony leaves for greens, they lend the elegance these lilies deserve. You will have the lovely wedding or reception complete with the fragrance of romance!

Summer from coast to coast is filled with flowers. California, Iowa, Ohio, and New York offer some of the finest roses in the country. You don't have to have many to arrange for a dinner party, but you should have a container that sets them apart. Two antique blue French Parian vases modeled with a hand clasping them are perfect for roses. Three are enough for each vase: the first a barely opened bud rising one and a half times the height of the vase; the second, half-open, about two inches below that; and the third almost spilling its full bloom over the rim. With the other container almost identical, the two give your dinner table the charming look of summer.

'Enchantment' lilies are at their best in August. They are especially attractive when they are arranged in glowing copper containers, as you can see in the picture on page 48c. This table shows that all arrangements don't have to be made with flowers. Here a skillful arrangement of summer fruit—lemons, limes, peaches, plums, kiwi, grapes, and

99

a whole pineapple—can echo the colors of the cloth and the flowers and add contrasting texture and form to the complete table.

September brings a new dimension in everyone's life. Summer ends, fall begins; kindergartens and universities take center stage; the air stirs with plans; Christmas is just around the corner!

No matter that September and October may produce hot days in Iowa or Colorado and even New Hampshire, the nights are cool, there's a threat of frost, and the decorator hastens to echo this new anticipation in the house.

Chrysanthemums

This is the season of chrysanthemums. In pots they will bring gold or lavender into the family room, where they will last for weeks. If you decide to have an informal supper party, chrysanthemums are the perfect flower to decorate your table. Use a copper bowl; this time wide, with a short-based pedestal, to hold bronze pompon chrysanthemums flanked by tall brass candlesticks with bright orange candles. If you have or can borrow a copper samovar to put at one end of the bare wood table to hold hot coffee and a fat brown pottery bowl for your special *chile con carne* at the other end, your table will be inviting to all.

And your arrangement of pompons will be hearty and handsome at least ten days after your guests have departed.

In Idaho and Wyoming, where frost comes early, this is the time to bring out your glycerinized pear branches, so smooth and silky-textured, and arrange them in your entrance hall with the deep red crested coxcomb as the focal point. You will be proud that you have created the "everlasting" foliage and flowers yourself.

September is also the month to use the old metal umbrella stand you bought at the auction to hold tall sunflowers that are at every roadside stand or in your own garden. Place it in front of your fireplace, which is not ready for warmer uses in the mild weather, and it will gleam as brightly as the outdoors.

In October in Wisconsin the bittersweet vine is ripening, either on your own gatepost or at the supermarket. If you happen to have inherited a beautiful wicker birdcage

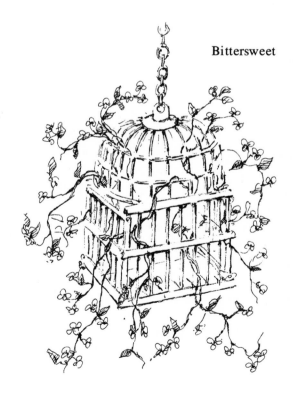

Bittersweet

(with no bird laying claim to it), this will be a marvelous decoration for your family room or even the dining room for the whole month. Below the ring in the center of the cage, wire the bright orange and yellow bittersweet berries and let long trailing branches of them hang down around the cage. The branches can be worked in between the wicker sides as if they were growing naturally there. No water is necessary. The cage can be covered with plastic when you're tired of looking at it and stored on a top shelf in the closet until next year. A very delightful and economical decoration!

In North Dakota, October is the time to bring the tall, dried tan *Allium,* dried cattails, and the wheat to make a monochromatic arrangement against the paneled walls of the living room. A simple, small-mouthed green or beige pottery vase will hold them handsomely. If you need some support for the thin stems, use #18 florist's wire across the opening of the vase, both ways, with each wire's ends bent securely over the lip of the opening. Your wheat must be the processed kind for arrangements. You can pull it into different lengths and bind it together securely with a Twist'em. The arrangement will look twice as impressive if you set it on a dark brown base.

Don't forget your own front door during these harvest months of October and November. With the colors trumpeting all around you, luring you to the woods or the mountains to see them, you're sure to find roadside markets full of pumpkins, Indian corn, strange-shaped and spotted gourds, and crimson apples. Make a colorful "welcome" arrangement on the outside of the front door. Hang it with denim ribbon or orange tape tied in a bow, to give a feeling of the season to all who pass by. Even a city apartment door deserves a decoration of bright gourds and little ears of red corn!

For Thanksgiving, you might decide to have an evening dinner for all your family. A yellow damask cloth would be lovely for your table, and you might want to try a different way to arrange your flowers. Find two round, shallow glass holders that slip over your two silver candlesticks (see page 33). Before you place them there, fill them with dry green ozite, which you can then saturate with water. Into these circular holders place your flowers—small yellow chrysanthemums with English ivy trailing over the edges or three longer-stemmed yellow snapdragons stretching out on both sides with short, bronze button chrysanthemums filling in around the candle. You can use any flower you wish and get an elegant effect with very few blossoms. Echo the yellow cloth with yellow candles and you will have a thankful Thanksgiving dinner table!

Now, with unbelievable speed, the year has rolled round to December. The pace is equaled by every family in every part of

101

the country. While there still is time, you and your family can make wreaths to decorate your home. Buy a form of green styrofoam, or find a fat metal circle stuffed with moss that you can soak and drain. Buy some evergreen branches: arborvitae, long-needled pine, cedar, yew. They keep their colors, which fir and balsam do not. Cut them into pieces 2 to 4 inches long, just big enough to tuck into your wreath. Stick pieces of one kind into the wreath about one-sixth of the way around, then change to another kind of green. After covering the same amount of space, change back to the first green. Halfway, change to a third green; at four-sixths, go back to the first kind; at five-sixths, change to a fourth green. Where a change of greens is made, you can wire a cluster of three cones to hide it. The wreath is now ready to hang on your door with whatever ribbon you want to attach to it. Keep some bags of pieces of cedar or arborvitae or whatever to replace any bits of green that might fall out.

Other charming decorations you and your family can make are small Christmas trees.

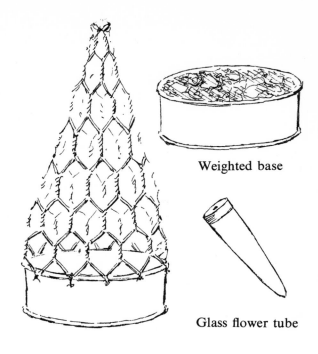

Weighted base

Glass flower tube

These are made of chicken wire with 1-inch openings, shaped into a cone about 9 inches tall. This has to be soldered to a metal base that is heavy enough to stand solidly. The bottom of a tuna fish can—4 inches in diameter and 1¼ inch deep—works fine. Put a few small stones in it, stir up homemade concrete, and pour it over the stones. This will make it completely steady. You can make two of these trees almost as easily as you can make one. Stuff each chicken-wire frame full of sphagnum moss, and when you're ready to make the trees, soak the moss thoroughly in the kitchen sink until it is completely moist. Meanwhile, order some ground pine from your florist or supermarket; that is the best material to use to make the trees. When you have that, stick the stems into the moistened moss inside the tree to make the finest shape you can imagine. It will be wider at the base and come to a point at the top. It is simple to keep the trees fresh by adding a little water to the

moss when it feels dry to your finger. When Christmas Eve comes, stud the trees with flowers. Carnations, red or pink, are the best, but if they are too expensive, geraniums, pink or red, will do. Buy some glass pointed tubes with rubber tops and a hole in the rubber from your florist. Fill the tube with water, put on the rubber top, cut your carnation to the size you want it, push the stem through the rubber top, and thrust the tube and flower inside your little tree. With about four blossoms circling the tree, and one at the top, you can have two darling Christmas trees for the price of ten flowers!

They will gladden your heart whenever you look at them. They will last all twelve days of Christmas, if you take the tubes out every few days, cut the flower stems a little, put fresh water in, and replace them. Year after year, the little trees will serve you—waiting patiently after New Year's Eve for the next Christmas.

Every family has special treasures that they bring out only at Christmas. It could be an old violin found in an antique shop in Pennsylvania—not to play but to hang on the owner's front door at Christmas with greens nestling under its strings and a green velvet ribbon supporting it on the door.

Everywhere the decorations of the homes are different, too. In the South the lovely wisteria vine is used to wreathe the staircase and the mantel. In Texas and Arizona, near the Mexican border, they use bougainvillea in the houses and borrow the Spanish custom of hanging the hollow paper image of human, animal, bird, or make-believe creature for children to play a game of hitting the *piñata* in turn. Whoever hits it gets the prize candy inside. In the Northwest there's the English holly. In Minnesota and Wisconsin, evergreen branches are made into swags. In Connecticut and Massachusetts there's American holly, growing outside and cut to decorate the house. In Kentucky they shoot mistletoe from the tall pecan trees to hang under each doorway to get a kiss from the pretty girls. In Mississippi there are still roses at Christmas. Florida grows white gladioluses. Hawaii hangs ti leaves and sprays of orchids.

These are some of the flowers and shrubs and vines that grow all over our fifty states, but from Maine to California you can find all of them, garnered, shipped, and used by everybody in every climate to say "Merry Christmas"!

No matter where you live, no matter what heritage you possess, each month of the year can bring you riches to decorate your home. Each season's beauty offers you the pleasure of discovery—seeing form, space, color, and texture in flowers and plants as you had never seen them before. Each of these pleasures brings you a self-awareness and confidence that produces, in its turn, a lasting happiness.

APPROXIMATE RANGE OF
AVERAGE ANNUAL MINIMUM
TEMPERATURES FOR EACH ZONE

ZONE 1   BELOW −50° F
ZONE 2   −50° TO −40°
ZONE 3   −40° TO −30°
ZONE 4   −30° TO −20°
ZONE 5   −20° TO −10°
ZONE 6   −10° TO 0°
ZONE 7   0° TO 10°
ZONE 8   10° TO 20°
ZONE 9   20° TO 30°
ZONE 10   30° TO 40°

Reprinted from "Plant Hardiness Zone Map," Miscellaneous Publication No. 814, published by the Agricultural Research Service, United States Department of Agriculture.

Appendix

Hibiscus

THE ZONES OF PLANT HARDINESS

The map on the opposite page shows in moderate detail the expected minimum temperatures in most of the horticulturally important areas of the United States (except Alaska and Hawaii) and Canada. It shows 10 different zones, each of which represents an area of winter hardiness for certain ornamental plants.

In determining if a certain plant will survive in a given zone, it is necessary to consider factors other than the minimum temperature range of each zone. For example, the temperatures of adjacent zones become increasingly similar near their common boundary. Moreover, there are innumerable island climates that may be considerably milder or colder than the zone average. These islands are especially frequent in hilly or mountainous areas. Mountainous areas on this map are not shown to be as cold as might be expected. The reason for this is that most weather stations from which records were obtained are located in valleys where temperatures tend to be somewhat milder, and where plants are most likely to be cultivated.

Other plant-growth factors must also be considered. Frost occurrence, seasonal rainfall distribution, humidity, soil characteristics, and duration and intensity of sunlight may bear little relationship to mean winter temperatures. The combined effects of all factors determine true plant adaptability. They would be difficult to depict geographically.

Minimum temperatures, on the other hand, can be readily depicted. They are of prime importance in plant survival. Their effects can seldom be changed by cultural practices.

105

Flowers—Annuals

Common Name	Horticultural	Zone(s)	Height	Color	When It Blooms	Where to Find It
African Daisy	*Arctotis grandis*	3–7	15–18 in.	White, yellow, red, violet	May–June	Nursery, super-market, florist, seed company
Ageratum	*A. houstonianum*	3–7	3–7 in.	Lavender blue, dark blue, white, pink	April or May till frost	Nursery, super-market, florist, seed company
Aster (China)	*Callistephus chinensis*	3–6	10–30 in.	Pink, blue, rose, white; no yellow	June till frost	Nursery, florist, seed company
Bachelor's Button or Cornflower	*Centaurea cyanus*	3–6	12–24 in.	Blue, purple, pink, white	June–July	Nursery, florist, seed company
California Poppy	*Eschscholzia californica*	3–7	12–15 in.	Yellow-orange; hybrids red, apricot, rose, red and white	March–September	Florist, seed company
Celosia	*C. plumosa* 'Red Fox'	3–8	2 ft.	Scarlet, carmine	July till frost	Nursery, florist, seed company
	'Golden Triumph'	3–8	2½ ft.	Golden yellow	July till frost	Nursery, florist, seed company
Chinese Pink	*Dianthus chinensis*	3–7	12–15 in.	Single and double, pink, white, red, coral	June–October	Nursery, florist, seed company
Cosmos	*C. bipinnatus*	3–6	5–9 ft.	Pink, rose, white	July till frost	Nursery, seed company
Coxcomb	*Celosia argentea cristata*	3–8	8 in.–2½ ft.	Red, apricot, gold, coral	July till frost	Nursery, florist, seed company
	'Fire Glow'	3–8	18 in.	Crimson, scarlet	July till frost	Nursery, florist, seed company
	'Toreador'	3–8	20 in.	Bright crimson red	July till frost	Nursery, florist, seed company
Dahlia	*D. variabilis*	7–10	1–2 ft.	White, yellow, pink, lavender, purple, red	July till frost	Nursery, seed company
Globe Amaranth	*Gomphrena globosa*	4–7	2 ft.	Red, pink, white, orange	July, August	Nursery, florist, seed company
Flowering Tobacco	*Nicotiana alata grandiflora*	3–7	3–4 ft.	White (fragrant), rose, pink, red	July till frost	Nursery, florist, seed company
Immortelle	*Xeranthemum annuum*	4–7	2–3 ft.	Pink, rose, red, purple, white	July till frost	Nursery, florist, seed company

CULTURE	WHEN TO CUT OR BUY	HOW TO CONDITION
Tolerant of poor soil and drought. Remarkably free from pests. Blooms all summer if fading flowers are removed.	Full bloom.	Has hollow stem. Put into scalding hot water for a minute to keep juice from running out. If flower wilts, revive it by putting in water again.
Dwarf varietal suitable for edging; easy to grow. Ordinary garden soil. Sun or partial shade.	Cut or buy when half the flowers in each head are open, the rest showing good color.	Take off leaves from lower stem. Put into deep, cool water as long as possible before arranging. Cut and change water daily. Should last at least a week.
Fertile soil, full sun, though some varieties will stand part shade. Requires ample moisture, not much cultivation. Many varieties.	They come in "early," "mid-season," or "late." Cut or buy in full bloom.	Take off leaves. Put into deep water at least one hour before arranging.
Hardy, vigorous. Likes poor, sandy soil. Leaves grow about 5 inches long. Goes to seed fast. Should be reseeded if grown in garden.	Full bloom. Cut dead blossoms off to promote more bloom.	Take off lower leaves. Put into deep water to condition.
Easy to grow if seed is sown where they are to flower. Light, sandy soil. If blossoms are cut off so no seed pods form, will bloom many months.	Full bloom. Lasts exceedingly well.	Take off lower leaves. Soak in deep water before arranging.
Same as Coxcomb.	Same as Coxcomb.	Same as Coxcomb.
Easy to grow in a sunny location with rich, rather moist soil. The F_1 hybrids are hardy, handsome. All are bushy plants.	Full bloom. Lasts well.	Take off lower leaves. Soak one hour before arranging.
Poor or indifferent soil. Full sun. Tall, thin stems. Profusion of leaves cut into threadlike pieces. Stake if in a windy spot.	Flowers can be single, double, or crested. Cut or buy when in full bloom. If in garden, cut off dead blooms to keep new ones blossoming.	Take off lower leaves. Soak stems in water one hour before arranging. Long-lasting.
Sow Coxcomb where you want it to grow, or buy plants ready to be set out. Easy to grow in reasonably rich soil. Needs moisture. Takes full sun and heat.	Buy from florist when available for cut flowers, or in fall as dried flowers. Cut to dry in your garden when bloom is full.	Take off lower and upper leaves. Put into cool water one hour before arranging. For drying: take off leaves; hang upside down in airy spot. Handsome. Long-lasting.
Likes fertile, reasonably moist soil, full sun. Start plants early indoors or sow directly outdoors.	Cut when in bloom.	Seal end of stem. To do this, put paper over a saucepan of scalding water and stick stem through the paper into the water. Hold it there for one minute.
Easy to grow in any soil. Endures drought and hot sun. Continuous bloom.	Can be found in fall at florist. Pick for drying when mature, about mid-August.	Hang upside down to dry. Color remains perfect. Long-lasting.
Easily grown. Will do well in shade. Transplants with ease, even in full flower, if done on a cloudy, moist day. Delicate fragrance.	Full bloom.	Remove lower leaves. Place in cool deep water one hour before arranging.
Hardy. Easy to grow in light, sandy soil. Full sun. Widely grown for winter arrangements. Silky, papery blooms.	Can be bought in fall at florist for dry bouquets. Cut before bloom is completely open for drying.	Hang upside down until bloom is dry.

107

Flowers—Annuals *(Continued)*

COMMON NAME	HORTICULTURAL	ZONE(S)	HEIGHT	COLOR	WHEN IT BLOOMS	WHERE TO FIND IT
Impatiens	*I. sultani*	3–7	6–15 in.	White, pink, coral, orange, red	June till frost	Nursery, florist, seed company
	I. holsti	3–7	16–25 in.	Same as *I. sultani*	June till frost	Nursery, florist, seed company
Larkspur	*Delphinium ajacis*	4–7	3–5 ft.	Blue, pink, rose, lilac, white	June–July	Nursery, florist, seed company
Love-Lies-Bleeding	*Amaranthus caudatus*	3–9	12–30 in.	White, blue, purple, rose, pink, salmon, yellow, red, patterned	July–August	Nursery, seed company
Marigold	*Tagetes*	3–9	6 in.–3 ft.	Yellow, gold, bronze, orange, white, bicolored	June till frost	Nursery, super-market, florist, seed company
Nasturtium	*Tropaeolum majus*	3–8	6–8 ft.	Yellow, red, orange	June till frost	Nursery, florist, seed company
	Tropaeolum minus	3–8	6–12 in.	Same as *T. majus*	June till frost	Nursery, florist, seed company
Petunia	*P. hybrida*	3–9	6–24 in.	All colors	May till frost	Nursery, florist, supermarket, seed company
Pot Marigold	*Calendula officinalis*	3–9	12–20 in.	Lemon, apricot, orange, gold	June till frost	Nursery, seed company, florist
Queen Anne's Lace	*Daucus carota*	3–7	18–30 in.	White	July–August	Wild
Salpiglosis	*Salpiglossis sinuata*	3–6	18–24 in.	Purple, yellow, red, variegated	June till frost	Nursery, florist, seed company
Salvia	*S. farinacea*	3–7	3 ft.	Blue bedder	July till frost	Nursery, florist, seed company
	S. splendens 'Evening Glow'	3–6	20 in.	Rose pink	July till frost	Nursery, florist, seed company
Scabiosa	*S. atropurpurea*	3–8	12–36 in.	White, blue, rose, pink, crimson, lavender	July till frost	Nursery, florist, seed company
Snapdragon	*Antirrhinum majus*	3–8	3 ft.	Orange, yellow, white, pink, red purple	All summer	Nursery, florist, seed company

CULTURE	WHEN TO CUT OR BUY	HOW TO CONDITION
One of the finest bedding plants for shady locations. Requires regular watering. Will not take low temperatures.	Buy or cut in full bloom or in pot for house plant.	Take off lower leaves. Put into cool water to condition before arranging.
Same as *I. sultani.*	Same as *I. sultani.*	Same as *I. sultani.*
Plants are hardy; can be sown in fall or spring. Takes full sun. Upright spires.	Full bloom. Greenhouse flower very beautiful.	Take off lower leaves. Put into cool water for one hour before arranging.
A tropical annual. Will stand poor, sandy soil, much heat and drought. Foliage brightly colored. Easily grown.	Cut when in bloom.	Easily dried by hanging upside down.
Tolerant of poor soil. Grows in sun or part shade. Easy to seed and transplant, even in flower.	Full bloom or bud.	Take off leaves. Put into cool water for one hour before arranging. Remove old blooms. Lasts long time. Dry well with Flower-Dri.
Easy to grow. Poor soil gives more bloom. *T. majus* is a vine; needs support.	Full bloom. Peel off dead blossoms to keep plant blooming.	Take off lower leaves. Condition in cool water. Bundle several flowers together—tie with twist'ems—arrange in groups.
Bushy. Full sun.	Same as *T. majus.*	Same as *T. majus.*
One of the most lovely and dependable flowers. Takes full sun or partial shade. Any kind of soil. Transplants well. Cut back if spindly; will thicken. Dwarf, tall, hanging, single, double.	Buy from florist when available. Cut in bud or full bloom. Take off spent blossoms to keep it blooming.	Take off lower leaves. Put into cool water one hour before arranging. Lasts long time.
Easy to grow in full sun. Any ordinary soil. Seed indoors or set out bought plants. For best flowers, pinch off all but center flower when in bud.	Buy from florist when available. Cut in full bloom. Long-lasting.	Set in cool water one hour before arranging. Wire and dry in Flower-Dri.
This "wild carrot" can be found growing in the country or near railroad tracks where land has not been disturbed by plowing or cropped by animals. Likes dry, sandy, sunny soil.	Cut this in all stages of bloom to dry for charming fall and winter bouquets.	Has cluster of blossoms and strong stem. Dry it with Flower-Dri for about 4 days.
Temperamental to raise. Full sun or partial shade in any soil, even poor soil. Flowers petunia-shaped. Gold marking in the throat. Exotic, unusual flower.	Full bloom.	Take off lower leaves. Put into cool water one hour before arranging. Long-lasting.
Perennial in southern states; annual in North. Easily grown; best in full sun, but will grow in partial shade. Does well in poor soil.	Wonderful flowers to arrange; very generous bloomers. Cut when in full bloom; buy whenever available at florist.	Take off lower leaves. Let stand in cool water one hour before arranging. Long-lasting blooms.
"All American" winner. Annual. Does best in sun; thrives in partial shade.	Same as *S. farinacea.*	Same as *S. farinacea.*
Hardy. Full sun. Ordinary soil. Long-season annual.	Buy when available; cut when in full bloom. Dwarf and giant varieties.	Let stand in cool water one hour before arranging.
Same as F₁ hybrids.	Available at florist almost all year.	Cut off lower leaves. Cut stems under water to revive blooms. Let stand in cool water at least one hour before arranging.

Flowers—Annuals *(Continued)*

COMMON NAME	HORTICULTURAL	ZONE(S)	HEIGHT	COLOR	WHEN IT BLOOMS	WHERE TO FIND IT
Snapdragon *(Continued)*	*A. m. F₁ hybrida* 'Rocket'	3–8	30–36 in.	Separate colors	June till frost	Nursery, florist, seed company
	A. m. F₁ hybrida 'Bright Butterflies'	3–8	24 in.	Mixed colors	June till frost	Nursery, florist, seed company
	A. m. F₁ hybrida 'Little Darling'	3–8	12 in.	Mixed colors	June till frost	Nursery, florist, seed company
Statice	*Limonium sinuatum*	4–9	12 in.–2½ ft.	White, yellow, blue, pink, lavender	August till frost	Nursery, florist, seed company
Stock	*Mathiola incana*	3–8	1–2½ ft.	White, rose, blue, lavender, purple, crimson	July till frost	Nursery, florist, seed company
	Mathiola incana #16	Greenhouse	2½ ft.	White	January–February	Florist
Strawflower	*Helichrysum bracteatum monstrosum*	4–7	30 in.	Red, purple, rose, salmon, yellow, white	July–August	Nursery, florist, seed company
	Helichrysum bracteatum original	3–8	30 in.	Mixed	July–August	Nursery, florist, seed company
Summer Cypress or Burning Bush	*Kochia scoparia trichophila*	4–8	2½ ft.	Green foliage, turns crimson	Insignificant	Nursery, florist, seed company
Sunflower	*Helianthus annuus*	3–8	1½–10 ft.	Golden yellow	July till frost	Nursery, florist, supermarket
Swan River Everlasting or Acroclinium	*Helipterum manglesii*	4–8	8–15 in.	White, pink, yellow center	July till frost	Nursery, seed company, florist
Sweet Pea	*Lathyrus odoratus*	3–6	4–6 ft.	Blue, purple, yellow, orange, red	June–July	Seed company, florist
Verbena	*V. hortensis*	3–8	8–15 in.	White, pink, red, salmon, lavender, blue, often with white eye	June till frost	Nursery, seed company, florist

CULTURE	WHEN TO CUT OR BUY	HOW TO CONDITION
Bred for garden and disease tolerance. Rich, mellow soil. Likes full sun, but will take partial shade.	Buy when available at florist; cut when lower flowers on stems are open. Available in separate colors. Blooms again when faded spikes are cut off.	Same as *Antirrhinum* hybrids.
Bred for round open-throat azalea-type blossoms. "All American" winner. Full sun or partial shade.	Buy when available; cut when in full bloom.	Same as *Antirrhinum hybrida*. Dries well with Flower-Dri.
"All American" winner azalea-type blossom. Sun or partial shade.	Buy when available; cut when in full bloom.	Same as *Antirrhinum* hybrids.
Not really Statice but listed as such in many catalogs. Easily grown. Likes sandy soil, full sun. Charming, dainty.	Buy whenever available from florist. Easy to cut and dry for "everlasting" flower. Some tall, some dwarf.	Doesn't need to be put into water. Hang upside down in garage or basement to dry. Lasts for months.
Plants difficult to grow well. Best to start seed indoors or buy seedlings to set out in garden when no danger of frost. Dwarf or tall varieties.	Order from florist whenever available; cut from garden when in full bloom.	Take off lower leaves. Cut stiff stem crosswise. Put into cool water one hour before arranging. Lasts well.
Special greenhouse variety.	Order in winter from florist.	Same as *M. incana*.
Any good soil. Sun. Good for beds. Excellent for drying. Double blossoms. Start seed indoors 6 weeks before warm weather. Moderately rich soil; full sun. Grown for foliage. Good for hedge or background.	Buy from florist in fall for dried blooms; cut in mid-August for house drying. Cut in August when foliage has turned red. Can be found at florist in fall for dried bouquets.	Hang upside down to dry in airy, cool spot. Lasts forever. Dry as fast as possible for fall and winter arrangements.
Same as *H. monstrosum*.	Same as *H. monstrosum*.	Same as *H. monstrosum*.
Start seed indoors 6 weeks before warm weather. Moderately rich soil; full sun. Grown for foliage. Good for hedge or background.	Cut in August when foliage has turned red. Can be found at florist in fall for dried bouquets.	Dry as fast as possible for fall and winter arrangements.
Will grow anywhere in sun, even in dry weather. A few varieties are dwarf. Some tall enough to serve as hedge or screen.	Buy whenever available; cut when in full bloom. Seeds are valuable as bird food in large varieties.	Pull off lower leaves. Cut large stems crosswise to take up water. Lasts long time. Dries well with Flower-Dri.
Daisylike; easy to grow. Full sun. Light, sandy soil.	Can be bought from florist in fall as dried flower. Cut when in full bloom.	Hang upside down until flower is dry. Handsome, everlasting.
Prepare bed in autumn or early spring, by deep digging and adding manure and compost. In spring (custom says on Good Friday) open trench 6 inches and place seed 4 inches apart. Cover with an inch of soil. Seed should be nicked and soaked 24 hours before planting. As your plants develop, the trench should be filled with earth until it is almost level. Wire is needed for vines to climb on. Don't let soil dry out.	Buy when flowers available at florist. Cut each day if grown at home, when bloom begins. Cool weather makes best flowering.	Let sweet peas condition in cool water at least one hour before arranging. Make bunch of same color, pull to height you desire, then bind together with twist'ems before arranging.
Dependable. Easy culture, spreading growth. Full sun. Transplants well. Dwarf and tall varieties.	Buy when available; cut when in full bloom. If dead blossoms removed, will bloom lavishly all summer.	Take off lower leaves. Let stand in cool water about one hour before arranging.

Flowers—Annuals *(Continued)*

Common Name	Horticultural	Zone(s)	Height	Color	When It Blooms	Where to Find It
Wheat	*Triticum aestivum*	2–5	4 ft.	Tawny gold	June–July	Wheatfields, florist
Zinnia	*Z. elegans*	3–9	8 in.–3 ft.	All colors except blue	June till frost	Nursery, florist, supermarket, seed company

Flowers—Biennials

Canterbury Bells or Cup-and-Saucer	*Campanula medium calycanthema*	3–7	2½ ft.	Blue, white, pink	South: March–April; North: June till frost	Nursery, florist
English Daisy	*Bellis perennis*	2–6	6 in.	Pink, rose, white	South: winter; North: May–July	Nursery, florist
Forget-Me-Not	*Myosotis alpestris*	3–7	6–12 in.	Blue, pink	April–June	Nursery, seed company, florist
Hollyhock	*Althaea rosea*	2–6	6–8 ft.	White, pink, rose, scarlet, yellow, crimson, purple	July–August	Nursery, seed company
Honesty	*Lunaria annua*	3–7	18–30 in.	White, silvery seed pods	June–July	Nursery, seed company
Pansy	*Viola tricolor hortensis*	3–7	6–8 in.	Blue, white, yellow, pink patterned	April–July	Nursery, seed company, florist, supermarket

Culture	When to Cut or Buy	How to Condition
	Can be cut from base of stem when it is ripe. Florists carry different sizes and from different countries. Buy in fall and winter.	Put wheat in tall vase to dry. Can be stored for use the following season.
Easiest possible culture. Can be started in house or outdoors from seed. Thrives best in sun, but will take partial shade. Transplants easily. Some varieties short-stemmed for border; some 3 feet tall with luxurious blossoms. Will survive drought and neglect and still add beauty to the garden.	Buy whenever available at supermarket or florist. Cut when in full bloom or when buds ready to open.	Take off lower leaves. Put into cool water for at least one hour before arranging. Very long-lasting. Dry, flat-leaved blossoms. Red color not satisfactory.
Seed must be planted in July and transplanted to cold frame in September. Protect from cold with mulch. In spring transplant to garden where bloom is wanted. Takes any soil as long as there is good drainage. Plants may be purchased from nursery in spring and set out in garden.	Buy in spring or summer when available at florist. Cut branches when in full bloom. Pick off dead blossoms on branches to keep flowers blossoming in garden.	Take off lower leaves. Put in cool water one hour before arranging.
Sow seeds in July for next-year bloom in moist, well-drained soil. Transplant to cold frame for winter protection in October. When trees leaf out in spring transplant where you want them to bloom. Or purchase young plants from nursery and set them in your garden. Prefers cool weather, not too hot sun.	Buy flowers from florist when available; cut in full bloom from your garden.	Same as Canterbury Bells.
Sow seed in July, transplant to beds or cold frame and in fall or spring to flowering locations.	Buy in spring when available; cut when in full bloom.	Take off lower leaves. Group six or eight stems of bloom together; hold with green floral tape or twist'em. Let stand in water for one hour, then arrange them in bunches in container.
Seed can be sown either in a cold frame or in the open ground in July or August for blooms the next year. Transplant to permanent location when it is small—early fall or early spring. Prefers full sun, but will take partial shade. Likes light, well-drained soil. Cut stalks as soon as blooms are gone.	Full bloom.	Take off lower leaves. Cut stems crosswise and let stand in water one hour before arranging.
Sow seeds in June or July where they are to remain. Partially shady. Cover with mulch first winter. They will bloom and set seed the next summer.	Cut after flowers fade and seed pods develop.	Hang upside down to dry, or stand in airy spot.
Seed should be started in July or August. Transplant into cold frame in garden where they can be covered with salt marsh hay or straw after ground freezes. Put wire around bed to keep out rabbits. Transplant in spring. Can be done even if plants are blooming. If dead blossoms and seed pods are kept off plants, flowers will bloom for months.	Buy whenever available; pick in bud or full bloom.	Condition leaves separately. Collect pansy stems in bunches of 5 or 7 flowers and tie them lightly with floral tape or twist'ems. Put into cool water in refrigerator for one hour, then arrange bunches in your container.

Flowers—Biennials *(Continued)*

COMMON NAME	HORTICULTURAL	ZONE(S)	HEIGHT	COLOR	WHEN IT BLOOMS	WHERE TO FIND IT
Sweet William	*Dianthus barbatus*	3–7	12–20 in.	Pink, salmon, red, mixed	June–July	Nursery, seed company, florist

Flowers—Perennials

African Lily	*Agapanthus africanus*	6–9	3 ft.	Blue	July–August in pot or bed; all summer in South	Nursery, florist
Baby's Breath 'Bristol Queen'	*Gypsophila paniculata*	3–8	18–30 in.	White	June–July	Nursery, florist
Balloon Flower	*Platycodon grandiflorum*	3–6	2 ft.	Blue, pink, white	June till frost	Seed company, florist
Bee Balm	*Monarda didyma*	2–6	3 ft.	Red, pink, white	June till frost	Seed company
Betony	*Stachys grandiflora*	3–6	18–30 in.	Violet-purple	June–July	Nursery, seed company
Blanket Flower	*Gaillardia aristata*	2–7	12–30 in.	Red, yellow, copper	June till frost	Seed company, florist
Carnation	*Dianthus caryophyllus*	9–10	2 ft.	Pink, red, white, mottled	Summer	Florist
Cattail	*Typha latifolia*	Everywhere	5–8 ft.	Brown	Spring till fall	Florist, wild
Chrysanthemum Garden mums Daisy mums Decorative mums Button mums Fuji mums	*C. morifolium* 'Cushion' 'Large Flowered Single' 'Large Flowered Double' 'Pompon' 'Spider'	3–7	15–36 in.	White, pink to red, yellow to bronze, lavender to purple	July till frost	Nursery, florist

CULTURE	WHEN TO CUT OR BUY	HOW TO CONDITION
Sow seed in June for the next year. Transplant into cold frame or in open garden in North, covering with marsh hay or straw after ground is frozen. In the South covering is not necessary. Transplant in early spring.	Buy whenever available; cut when in full bloom.	Take off lower leaves. Cut stiff stems crosswise. Stand in cool water one hour before arranging. Long-lasting.
Hardy in warm, sunny climates. Otherwise it can be grown in pots or put into the garden in May and taken out before frost. Very handsome and elegant.	When blossom is almost completely open.	Take off any lower foliage and put the stem of the flower into deep, cool water in a cool room for at least half a day. It should last at least a week after it is conditioned.
Light, well-drained soil. Full sun. Set purchased plants where you want them in April or October, 2–3 feet apart. Stake when in bloom.	Can be bought at florist almost all year round. Cut in garden when in full bloom.	Take off lower leaves. Set in cool water one hour before arranging. Hang upside down to dry for fall and winter use.
Hardy; long-lived. Sandy, well-drained soil. Full sun. Does not like transplanting.	Cut when top flower is in bloom; others will open.	Needs to be seared on the stem as soon as it is cut. Do this with candle held under stem. Put into cool water to condition. Whenever stem is taken out and recut, it must be seared again.
Often grown as an herb. Grows in shade as well as sun. Blooms all summer. Takes any soil.	Cut or buy when one-quarter of the blooms on a stem are half open.	Remove bottom leaves on stem. Put into deep, cool water, overnight if possible. Should last a week; buds and foliage last even longer.
Start from seed in house in February. Or buy plants to set out in April or October. Full sun. Good rich soil with moisture, but well drained. Divide clumps every 2 or 3 years.	Full bloom.	Take off lower leaves. Let stand in cool water one hour before arranging.
Does not mind poor soil. Loves sun and heat. Takes drought.	Buy when available; cut when in full bloom. Dwarf and tall varieties.	Remove bottom leaves on stem. Put into deep, cool water, overnight if possible. Should last a week; buds and foliage last even longer.
Not hardy where winters are severe. Full sun. Ordinary garden soil except an acid one. If acid, add a teaspoon of lime to each plant, mixed with soil. For best blooms take off all but one bud to each stem.	Buy at florist whenever available; cut from garden when flower is in full bloom.	Remove bottom leaves. Cut below node of stem. Let stand in cool water one hour before arranging. Long-lasting.
Native wild plant grows in low, wet marshes and streams. Not recommended to grow in your garden!	Dry cattails, short or long, can be bought at florist in autumn. If cut in the wild, do before July 4 or the tail will come apart.	Do not put into water. Let stand in a tall vase until dried. Can be stored for use the next season.
Light, rich, well-drained soil. Full sunlight. Set plants out in spring. Pinch back after 3 or 4 leaves have formed. Pinch a second time in early July. Feed in early spring and every week until bloom comes. Mulch during winter. In spring when the plants begin to grow they should be lifted, divided, and one shoot replanted.	Almost always available at florists, either in cut variety or in pots. In the garden cut either in full bloom or when the top blossoms are almost ready to open completely.	Take off the lower leaves of the chrysanthemum stem. Split the woody stem crosswise, then let stand in cool water at least one hour before you arrange them. Long-lasting. Can be dried with Flower-Dri.

Flowers—Perennials *(Continued)*

COMMON NAME	HORTICULTURAL	ZONE(S)	HEIGHT	COLOR	WHEN IT BLOOMS	WHERE TO FIND IT
Columbine	*Aquilegia hybrida*	3–7	2 ft.	Blue, pink, rose, purple, yellow, white, combinations of colors	June till frost	Florist, seed company
Coral Bells	*Heuchera sanguinea*	3–8	12–20 in.	Red, pink	June till frost	Florist, seed company
Cupid's Dart	*Catananche caerulea*	4–8	12–18 in.	Blue	June–August	Seed company, florist
Daylily	*Hemerocallis* hybrids	3–6	12 in.–3 ft.	Lemon to orange, pink to red, lavender to purple, mottled	Early–late summer	Seed company
Delphinium	*D. hybridum* 'Pacific Hybrids'	3–6	4–8 ft.	Pink shades, deep blue, mid-blue, pale blue, white, violet, double blooms with contrasting or matching bees (centers)	June, again in August	Seed company, florist
	'Connecticut Yankee'	3–6	2 ft.	White, light blue, single	June; all summer	Seed company, florist
Edelweiss	*Leontopodium alpinum*	4–5	5–7 in.	Pearly white	June	Nursery, seed company
Gas Plant	*Dictamnus albus*	3–6	3 ft.	Pink, white	June–July	Seed company
Geranium	*Pelargonium hortorum*	3–9	12–20 in.	White, pink, rose, coral, red, salmon, crimson	May till frost; in frost-free climates, all year	Seed company, supermarket, florist
Iris	*Iris,* bearded hybrids	3–7	12–20 in.	White, yellow, orange, pink, red, blue, purple, combinations	May–July	Seed company, supermarket, florist
Lantana	*L. camara*	8–9 along coasts	18–30 in.	Orange, white yellow, red	All year	Seed company
Leopard's Bane	*Doronicum plantagineum*	2–6	18–30 in.	Bright yellow	April–May	Seed company

116

CULTURE	WHEN TO CUT OR BUY	HOW TO CONDITION
Rich, well-drained soil. Sun or partial shade.	Buy whenever available at florist. Cut when half flowers are in full bloom. Keep dead flowers and seed pods off branches to encourage more bloom.	Take off lower leaves. Let stand in cool water before arranging. Long-lasting.
Wonderful in garden. Long-lived; graceful. Likes part shade, sun.	If you grow it, cut when half the spray is in bloom. Buds won't open once they are cut.	Put flower into cool, deep water for as long as you can before arranging it. Change water each day, and recut stem.
Often grown as annual. Ordinary soil. Likes dry condition. Florists carry it as dry flower.	Buy in fall from florist for dry arrangements; cut when in bloom.	Combine stems. Hang upside down to dry. Only blue "everlasting."
Will grow in every state. Immune to heat. Completely hardy. Sun or partial shade. Likes sandy soil, but will thrive even in poor soil as long as it has good drainage.	Most blossoms last only a day, but will be replaced with another flower the next day. Latest hybrids stay open almost 24 hours. Cut when lower blooms are open; others will open in arrangement.	Condition foliage in separate containers. Sear boom of stalk with candle flame before arranging, to keep fluid inside stem.
Set out in fall or spring. Takes some shade, rich feeding, and moisture. Needs to be staked early in growth. After bloom, cut the stalks halfway; when new growth begins, cut the old stalks to ground.	Make sure about half the flowers on the stalk are open.	Take off lower leaves and condition them separately. Put into deep, cool water in cool room at least overnight. Flowers should last at least a week. Do not crowd in container. These are royalty!
Same as 'Pacific Hybrids' but does not have to be cut down. Blooms all summer.	Same as 'Pacific Hybrids'. Be sure dead blooms and pods are taken off stems, to keep flowers blooming.	Same care as for 'Pacific Hybrids'. Change water each day and cut stems to be sure the water can get through the flower.
Rock garden; pretty loose soil with lime added. Set out purchased plants in October. Give light straw mulch.	Cut when in bloom for drying.	Hang upside down to dry. Lasts long time when dry.
Set purchased plant in rich garden soil in full sun. Does not like to be transplanted. Lasts forever. Strange lemony fragrance. Supposed to give off "gas" that can be ignited by a match on windless days.	Cut long stems when fully blossomed. Looks like single delphinium blossom.	Take off lower leaves. Cut stem crosswise and let sit in water one hour before arranging.
Can be grown from seed or bought from greenhouse or supermarket and transplanted into garden or window box. Not too rich soil. Full sun. See Potted Plants.	Available at greenhouse from spring to fall. Cut when in bud or full bloom.	Condition leaves separately. Let stems soak in cool water for at least one hour before arranging. Very long-lasting. Leaves are excellent greens for other flowers. Wire and dry with Flower-Dri.
Plant in sunny location. Well-drained soil; does well in heavy clay or sandy soil. Will take hot weather and cold winters. Divide every third year after blooming. In autumn, cut back foliage to about 4 or 5 inches. Plant in early August.	Buy at florist when available. Cut when lower blossom on stalk is open; others will open in arrangement.	Condition foliage separately. Let stalk sit in cool water one hour before arranging. Foliage can be glycerinized. Pull off dead blossoms and cut stems daily.
Tropical shrub used as bedding plant. Will not stand frost; set potted plants out in full sun in rather poor soil.	Buy potted plants from florist or nursery any time in tropical zones or in summer in cooler climate.	Used only as bedding plants.
Grow from seed or buy plants to set out in October. Full sun or partial shade. Rich soil with moisture but good drainage. Leaves disappear during summer, come back in fall.	Full bloom.	Take off lower leaves. Let stand in cool water before arranging.

117

Flowers—Perennials *(Continued)*

COMMON NAME	HORTICULTURAL	ZONE(S)	HEIGHT	COLOR	WHEN IT BLOOMS	WHERE TO FIND IT
Marsh Marigold	*Caltha palustris*	4–8	10–20 in.	Golden yellow	April–June	Wild, nursery
Oriental Poppy	*Papaver orientale*	3–7	3–4 ft.	Red, pink, rose, salmon, white	May–June	Nursery, seed company
Patent Leather Flower	*Anthurium andraeanum*	9–10	1–2 ft.	Red	Tropical, all year	Nursery, florist
Pearly Everlasting	*Anaphalis margaritacea*	3–8	18–30 in.	Pearl white	July–August	Seed company, wild, florist
Peony	*Paeonia hybrida*	3–6	15–36 in.	Pink, rose, red, white	May–June	Seed company, florist
Phlox	*P. paniculata*	3–8	18–36 in.	White, pink to red, lavender to purple, colored eye or solid	June–September	Nursery
Primrose English	*Primula vulgaris*	3–7	6 in.	White, yellow, pink, blue, lavender	April–May	Nursery
Polyanthus	*Primula polyantha*	3–7	8–12 in.	Yellow to orange, blue to purple, white	May–June	Nursery
Prickly Thrift	*Acantholimon glumaceum*	3–8	4–6 in.	Rose, pink	July–August	Nursery, florist

CULTURE	WHEN TO CUT OR BUY	HOW TO CONDITION
Hardy wild flower growing in marshes or alongside brooks. Easily transplanted into rich, moist soil if given partial shade.	Full bloom.	Let sit in cool water one hour before arranging. Lasts long.
Any good garden soil, light and sandy. Full sun. Cut stalk before seeds form. Plant becomes dormant and leaves disappear after bloom. Begins to grow again in August which is time to plant the flower. Has a long taproot, so dig a hole deep enough to hold it without breaking it. Mulch in winter. Stake stem before it blooms.	Cut from garden when bud is almost ready to open.	Sear stem of poppy with candle flame as soon as you cut it to keep liquid from running out. Then place it in deep cool water one hour before arranging. Whenever you cut stems, sear it again.
South American flower grown as pot plant. Lots of water and humidity. Rich soil, lots of light. Long heart-shaped green leaves. Brilliant, leathery orange-red flower, 4–6 inches long.	Plant and stems of flowers can be purchased.	Let stems sit in cool water before arranging.
Only American "everlasting." Grows anywhere in sandy soil. Wild plants easy to transplant.	Buy in fall from florist for dry arrangements. Cut from own plants when in bloom.	Hang upside down to dry. Everlasting.
Plant roots in September or October in full sun or partial afternoon shade. Soil should not be acid; a clay loam, well drained, is excellent. Dig hole about 18 inches deep, fill with 6 inches of fertilizer and topsoil. Place roots so that tops are almost 2 inches below surface. Fill with soil, firm down, and water. In spring, plants usually need support with iron rings around stems. In fall, cut stems just below soil; burn leaves and stems to prevent spreading of disease. Peonies do not like to be moved. They will last 25 years or more if left undisturbed. Many varieties: single, double, Japanese. Study in catalog.	Cut in bud, half opened, or fully opened. Buy whenever available at florist.	Take off leaves. Condition these separately. Split stems crosswise. Let sit in cool water as long as possible before arranging. Very perfumed, long-lasting. Leaves are handsome with different flowers.
Set out plant in fall or spring. Rich soil, good drainage. Sun or partial shade. Feed with high-potash fertilizer. Divide every 4 or 5 years.	Cut when bloom is open. Take off dead blooms so plant will keep on blooming. Don't cut too much off plant.	Pull off lower leaves. Cut stems crosswise to condition.
Set out plants in deep or partial shade in September or October. Likes rich woodsy soil. Can be divided and transplanted right after they flower.	Full bloom.	Take off lower leaves. Let sit in cool water one hour before arranging.
Much easier to grow than any other *Primula*. Can be set out in March as well as October; likes partial shade and rich, moist soil. Sometimes does not survive a second season.	Full bloom.	Same as *P. vulgaris*.
Related to Thrift. Needs gritty soil, full sun. Good for rock garden. Evergreen foliage.	Buy in fall from florist for dry arrangement. Cut when in bloom for drying.	Hang upside down in cool spot for drying. Charming one-sided blossoms.

Flowers—Perennials *(Continued)*

COMMON NAME	HORTICULTURAL	ZONE(S)	HEIGHT	COLOR	WHEN IT BLOOMS	WHERE TO FIND IT
Rose (Hybrid Tea)						
'Sonia'	*Rosa*	3–10	2½ ft.	Coral	All roses: June till frost	All roses: nursery, florist
'Bridal White'	*Rosa*	3–10	2½ ft.	White with rose blush		
'Golden Wave'	*Rosa*	3–10	2½ ft.	Gold		
'Peace'	*Rosa*	3–10	2½ ft.	White to ivory, gold at base		
Rose (Floribunda)						
'Sunset'	*Rosa*	3–10	2 ft.	Yellow		
'Mary Devore'	*Rosa*	3–10	2 ft.	Red		
Sea Lavender	*Limonium latifolium*	4–7	15–24 in.	Lavender	August–September	Nursery, florist
Shasta Daisy	*Chrysanthemum maximum*	3–6	15–30 in.	White	June–August	Seed company, florist, supermarket
Summer Salvia	*S. farinacea*	7–9	3 ft.	Blue	June till frost; all year in tropics	Seed company, florist, nursery
Thrift	*Armeria maritima*	3–8	6 in.	Pink, purple, white	June–July	Nursery, florist
Transvaal Daisy	*Gerbera*	4–8	24–32 in.	Orange, red, scarlet, pink, yellow, white, salmon	July till frost; tropical, all year	Seed company, florist
Tree Peony	*P. suffruticosa*	3–6	4–6 ft.	Red, white, lilac, yellow	May–June	Seed company
Violet	*Viola palmata*	2–8	3–7 in.	Violet, purple	April–June	Nursery, wildflower company
Wild Ginger	*Asarum canadense*	2–6	4–8 in.	Green leaf, brownish-purple flower	Flowers insignificant	Wildflower nursery

CULTURE	WHEN TO CUT OR BUY	HOW TO CONDITION
All roses: Roses must have sun at least half the day. Plant in spring or fall in rich garden soil. Dig large hole, 12 inches deep. Put in topsoil and old manure or compost; mix well. Plant with roots outstretched and head or crown about 2 inches below surface. Fill about 4 inches of soil over roots, then pour half bucket of water in. Let it settle. Fill hole with soil, then tamp soil firmly. Pull ground up over stem, to prevent drying out, for 2 weeks if planted in spring. In fall planting, leave soil on stem all winter. In southern and tropical climates roses don't require winter protection. Where there is hard frost and low temperatures in winter, all roses need protection. There are about 12 classifications of roses. Get a catalog and study their differences.	All roses: Order from florist all year. Cut from bush in bud or just before half-bloom.	All roses: Take off thorns. Cut stems slantwise with sharp knife. Put rose into cool water in cool room or refrigerator overnight before arranging. Change water each day. Cut stem slantwise each day.
Light, sandy soil. Full sun. Set purchased plants in April or October. Often called Statice incorrectly.	Buy in fall from florist as dried flowers; cut in garden in bloom.	Can be arranged fresh in cool water or hung upside down to dry for fall and winter arrangements.
Full sun. Good rich soil, well drained. Comes single and double. Learn varieties from catalog. Tends to die out every 2 or 3 years and needs to be replaced. Can be dried well.	Buy when available at florist; cut in full bloom.	Let sit in cool water one hour before arranging. Long-lasting. For drying, wire and dry face up in Flower-Dri.
Sow seed indoors or buy seedlings. Transplant after frost. Likes full sun, will take partial shade. Perennial in zones 8 and 9, annual elsewhere. Grows well in any type of soil.	But whenever available at florist; cut in full bloom.	Take off lower leaves. Let sit in cool water before arranging. Long-lasting. Dries well.
Sometimes called 'Statice Armeria'. Evergreen foliage. Set out purchased plants in April or October. Good in rock garden with light, sandy soil. Winter mulch with straw.	Buy dried flowers in fall from florist. Cut when in bloom for drying.	Excellent everlasting. Hang upside down in cool, airy spot. Color lasts well.
Not hardy north of Washington, D.C. Set potted seedling outside only when weather is warm. Full sun. Hardy in mild climates.	Florists can usually supply these flowers. Cut in garden when in full bloom.	Let sit in cool water before arranging.
Deciduous shrub. Should not be cut down in fall when leaves fall off. Prefers deep, sandy soil, in full sun with good drainage. Plant either in spring or fall at least 6 inches below surface. Lives many years. Beautifully shaped shrub in winter.	Blooms are single, semi-double, or fully double. Flowers are from 6–10 inches across. Cut sparingly to shape of shrub.	Condition leaves separately. Peel bark of stem up an inch, cut stem crosswise, and let sit in cool water at least one hour before arranging.
Will grow in partial shade or sun. Likes moist location. Plant in spring or fall.	Pick when in bloom.	Condition leaves separately. Combine violets in small bunches with floral tape. Set in cool water or refrigerate one hour before arranging.
Wildflower grown as a ground cover for its beautiful leaves, which are heart-shaped. Needs shade and moisture and humus in the soil. Set out plants in spring or fall.	Cut leaves whenever you want to use them as decorative greens.	Let sit in cool water or in refrigerator one hour before arranging. Lasts long time. Very handsome.

121

Flowers—Perennials *(Continued)*

COMMON NAME	HORTICULTURAL	ZONE(S)	HEIGHT	COLOR	WHEN IT BLOOMS	WHERE TO FIND IT
Winged Everlasting	*Ammobium alatum grandiflorum*	3–8	3 ft.	White	June–July	Seed company, florist
Yarrow	*Achillea filipendulina*	2–6	2–4 ft.	Golden yellow	July till frost	Seed company, florist, supermarket

Herbs

COMMON NAME	HORTICULTURAL	ZONE(S)	HEIGHT	COLOR OF FOLIAGE	BLOOMS OR FRUITS	WHERE TO FIND IT
Aloe	*A. variegata*	8–10	8 in.	Green, marbled white	Once or twice a year; scarlet flower	Nursery, florist
Basil 'Dark Opal'	*Ocimum basilicum*	3–7	15 in.	Deep purple, bronze	Insignificant	Nursery, seed company, florist
Chives	*Allium schoenoprasum*	2–7	10 in.	Green	Midsummer; pink-lavender flower	Nursery, seed company, florist
Lavender	*Lavendula spica*	3–8	2–3 ft.	Gray-green	June–July; light lavender, blue flower	Nursery, seed company
Lemon Balm	*Melissa officinalis*	3–7	1–2 ft.	Green	Insignificant	Nursery, seed company
Marjoram (Sweet)	*Origanum marjorana*	3–7	2 ft.	Green	July; white or purple spikes of flowers	Nursery, seed company
Mint (Spearmint)	*Mentha spicata*	3–8	1–2 ft.	Green	July; purplish flower	Nursery, seed company
Parsley	*Petroselinum crispum*	3–7	6–10 in.	Green	Insignificant	Nursery, seed company, supermarket
Rose Geranium	*Pelargonium graveolens*	4–8	2–3 ft.	Green	Summer; rose-pink flower	Nursery, florist, seed company
Rosemary	*Rosmarinus officinalis*	4–8	3–6 ft.	Green	July, August; pale blue, white flower	Nursery, florist
Summer Savory	*Satureja hortensis*	4–8	1–1½ ft.	Green	Insignificant	Nursery, seed company
Tarragon	*Artemisia dracunculus*	4–8	3 ft.	Green	Insignificant	Nursery, seed company
Teucrium	*T. chamaedrys*	3–7	12 in.	Green	July; rosy purple flower	Nursery

CULTURE	WHEN TO CUT OR BUY	HOW TO CONDITION
Perennial in mild climates, often grown as annual. Light, sandy soil. Full sun.	Buy in fall, dried from florist. Cut before mature for dying.	Combine cut stems. Hang upside down in shady cool place. Will hold white color indefinitely.
Easily grown. Likes sun. Any garden soil. Set plants out in April or October. Divide and replant every third year.	Buy in summer; cut when in full bloom.	Take off lower leaves. Cut stems crisscross. Long-lasting. Dries well.

CULTURE	WHEN TO CUT OR BUY	HOW TO CONDITION
A succulent, long-lived in pot. Otherwise for mild, dry climates with no frost. Takes sun. Sandy soil. Juice in leaves is remedy for burns.	Buy whenever florist can furnish it. Flowers are insignificant.	Grown as medicinal herb. Keep in kitchen in case of burns.
'All America' winner. Sunny spot, well-drained soil. Annual. Fragrant.	Buy whenever florist can furnish it. Ornamental in flower-bed. Cut when needed.	Take off lower leaves; arrange as colorful foliage.
Full sun. Dry, good soil. Divide every 3 or 4 years.	Any time from spring to frost.	For eating, not arranging.
Perennial. Full sun, any soil, good drainage. Needs coverings in winter to keep it from freezing.	Cut for drying just before full bloom.	Take off leaves. Set in cool water before arranging. Long-lasting.
Perennial. Grows in sun and any soil. Plant it in a plastic bag to keep it under control.	Cut or buy whenever you want to add this to your arrangement.	Strip the foliage at the base of the plant. Put into cool water or refrigerator for one hour, then arrange it. Cut stem and put new water in every other day.
Annual. Takes sun, any soil.	Buy whenever you want it. Gather to dry before it flowers.	Take off leaves. Set in cool water before arranging. Long-lasting.
Partial shade, plenty of moisture. Plant it in a plastic bag to keep it under control. Keep pruned. Perennial.	Cut early.	Same as Marjoram.
Biennial. Full sun. Prefers moist soil. Sometimes hard to start from seed. Buy plants in early spring. Cut out blossom. In warm zone, plant will often winter over.	Buy at supermarket all year. Cut from own plants all summer.	Wash and put in water in refrigerator.
Buy plants to set out after frost. Shrub in South, pot plant in North. Full sun, good soil. Will not take frost.	Cut leaves as needed.	When branch is cut for arrangement, condition leaves separately. Lasts long time.
Perennial. Evergreen. Set purchased plant in full sun in either April or October. Not hardy north of New York City. Should be grown in a pot and taken in before frost.	Don't cut branches. Take fragrant leaves as needed.	Not effective in arrangements.
Annual. Sunny location. Any good soil.	Cut leaves as needed.	Not effective in arrangements. Dries well.
Perennial. Prefers light shade, good soil. Difficult to grow from seed. Set out small plants or rooted cuttings.	Cut leaves as needed.	Not effective in arrangements. Dries well.
Perennial. Sunny or light shade. Easily rooted or divided.	Cut any time.	Not effective in arrangements.

Bulbs, Corms, and Tubers

COMMON NAME	HORTICULTURAL	ZONE(s)	HEIGHT	COLOR	WHEN IT BLOOMS	WHERE TO FIND IT
Allium or Ornamental Onion	*A. giganteum*	2–7	4–5 ft.	Violet-blue	June	Nursery, bulb company, florist
Begonia, Tuberous rooted	*B. tuberhybrida*	3–8	8–12	White, yellow, red, orange, pink	July till frost	Nursery, bulb company, florist
Canna	Giant hybrids	3–9	4–6 ft.	White, red, pink, yellow	July till frost	Bulb company, florist
	Dwarf hybrids	3–9	3 ft.	Pink, salmon, coral	July till frost	Bulb company, florist
Cyclamen	*C. persicum*	*See* House Plants chart				
Dahlia	*D.* hybrids Formal, informal, decorative cactus, semi-cactus	3–9	3–6 ft.	Red, rose, pink, yellow, white	June till frost	Bulb company, florist
	Unwin hybrid 'Redskin'	3–9	12–14 in.	Rich mixture of red colors	June till frost	Nursery, seed company
Dutch Iris	*Iris Xyphium*	4–8	18–24 in.	Blue, mauve, yellow, white	April–May	Nursery, florist, bulb company
Gladiola	*Gladiolus* hybrids	3–9	2–3 ft.	White, yellow, red, blue, green, combinations	July till frost	Bulb company, florist
Grape Hyacinth	*Muscari armeniacum*	2–8	3 in.	Blue	April–May	Bulb company
Hyacinth	*H. orientalis*	3–9	10–15 in.	White, pink, blue, yellow, rose	April–May	Florist, bulb company

CULTURE	WHEN TO CUT OR BUY	HOW TO CONDITION
Very hardy. Will grown in any good soil. Plant in fall.	Full bloom.	Put this tall-stemmed flower into cool, deep water for half a day before you arrange it. You will get great pleasure just looking at it. After it turns beige, hang it upside down to dry for the fall and winter.
Start tubers in February on peat moss, where roots develop and leaves appear. Transplant into 5-inch pot. Put outside where weather is warm. Needs partial shade to bloom best.	Buy from florist in spring; cut blooms when they are fully open.	Condition in cool water before arranging. Can be floated in water.
Bulbs planted in May. Foliage luxuriant. After frost, dry clumps and store over winter. May be left in ground in south.	Buy when available at florist; cut in bud or full bloom.	Condition leaves separately. They are handsome with other flowers too. Put flowers in cool water at least one hour before arranging. Cut stem and change water daily.
Dwarf cannas grown same way as giant hybrids, but easier in small garden.	Same as Giant Canna.	Same as Giant Canna.
Grow from tubers in rich, sandy garden soil. Plant in May. Must have good drainage. If best blooms wanted, pinch out all but one stalk. Stake it for protection. After frost, cut down to 6 inches, let stand a week, then dry tubers to store during winter.	Buy when florist offers them; cut when bloom is completely open.	Stem is wide and hollow and has to be sealed. Place stem in very hot water for one minute before arranging.
Grows from seed started indoors in April or bought from nursery. Bronze foliage, blooms all summer from compact bushy plant. "All-America" selection.	All summer.	Take off lower leaves. Let stand in cool water before arranging. Dry well with Flower-Dri.
Grown from a bulb outdoors or forced indoors. Takes full sun, ordinary garden soil. After bloom, let foliage dry, then lift bulbs and store them in hot attic. If flowers are cut, bulbs may need to be replaced next fall.	Buy in spring from florist. Cut own flowers when in full bloom, either forced indoors or growing outdoors.	Let stalks sit in cool water one hour before arranging. Condition foliage separately.
Plant after frost, in intervals of two weeks for longer blooming. Prefers sun, moderate moisture. After bloom, foliage turns yellow. Cut stalks 2 inches from ground. Lift corms out and let ripen on flats before storing for winter in cool room.	Buy from florist whenever available. Cut in garden as soon as one or two flowers show color. The blooms will open in water in your house.	Cut slantwise. Condition leaves separately. Let flower stems stand in cool water at least half a day before arranging. As flowers fade, remove. Cut stem again and arrange. Lasts long time.
Easy bulbs to grow. Sunny situation. Prefers rich, sandy soil. Plant in September or October. Forces easily in fall.	Full bloom.	Let stand in cool water or in refrigerator one hour before arranging. Lasts long time.
Reasonably hardy. Plant middle of September, about 5 to 6 inches underground in rich soil. In North, a mulch after freezing gives protection. Plant in clumps rather than straight lines. Fertilize after blooming. Forces easily if potted in October.	Buy at florist in spring; cut for home decorating when bloom is full.	Put in shallow container of water. Cut stem daily and add fresh water. Lasts long time.

Bulbs, Corms, and Tubers *(Continued)*

COMMON NAME	HORTICULTURAL	ZONE(S)	HEIGHT	COLOR	WHEN IT BLOOMS	WHERE TO FIND IT
Lily	*Lilium* species	3–8	1–6 ft.	White, yellow, crimson, spotted, varied	May till frost	Florist, bulb company
	Lilium hybrids	3–8	3–6 ft.	White, pink, silver, crimson, orange, gold, green, spotted, banded	May till frost	Bulb company, florist
Lily-of-the-Valley	*Convallaria majalis*	3–8	6–8 in.	White	May, June	Bulb company, florist
Narcissus	*Narcissus* hybrids	3–9	8–15 in.	White, yellow, pink, orange, gold, bicolored	March–May	Bulb company, florist
Narcissus, 'Paperwhite'	*N. tazetta*	Indoor forcing	12–15 in.	White	November–December	Florist, bulb company

Culture	When to Cut or Buy	How to Condition
Needs rich soil and excellent drainage. Can be planted spring or fall. Should have mulch in winter for protection, and in summer to keep roots cool. Needs sunny, airy location. Many species neither hardy nor disease-resistant.	Buy at florist whenever available, or ask florist to order blooming stalks from special lily growers. When you cut your own lilies, do not take more than two-thirds of stalk or bulb will suffer from loss of leaves for next season's bloom. Cut when lower blossoms are open and taller ones still in bud. They will open in arrangement. Pinch out stamen to prevent discoloration on blossom or furniture.	Remove lower leaves from stem. Place in deep, cool water at least one hour before arranging. Cut stems daily and add fresh water. Lily stalk will last a week or 10 days.
Hybrid lilies are hardier, taller, healthier than many species. They have been classified into 5 varieties according to their parentage. Study them in lily catalogs to see color, shape, and time of bloom. All lily bulbs should be planted with 4 inches of soil between the top of the bulb and the ground. Certain hybrids can be planted in containers outdoors or forced indoors. Remove all dead blossoms to prevent seeds forming. Do not cut stems down until after frost.	Same as *L.* species.	Same as *L.* species.
Primarily a shade plant. Tolerates half-shade but does best under shady trees. Plant "pips" in autumn, in rich soil supplied with humus and plenty of moisture. White, nodding bells are very fragrant. After 3 years, should be lifted, divided, and replanted.	Buy whenever available at florist; cut from your bed when in full bloom. The fragrance will fill your house.	Condition leaves separately. Tie 7 or 8 stalks together with green floral tape or twist'ems. Let stand in water in refrigerator for one hour, then arrange.
Hybrid narcissuses are divided into 8 divisions according to the size and shape of the flowers. Look at catalogs to learn colors and time of each division. May be grown in any kind of soil, especially sandy with good drainage. Will grow at edge of shrubbery and beneath trees. Plant in September or October. Small bulbs, 1–3 inches deep; large ones, 6 inches deep. Cut down stalks when bloom is finished, but don't cut down foliage until it has turned yellow and died down, otherwise bulbs will not bloom next season. Foliage can be braided or turned over into an upright mass and held with rubber bands until ready to be removed. Bonemeal can be worked into soil in autumn for fertilizer. These bulbs can be forced indoors in pots of soil to bloom from January to April.	Buy at florist in February and March; cut from your garden when full blossom or bud.	Put in cool water one hour before arranging. Shallow water is best. Condition foliage separately.
Paperwhites are ordered in fall from nurseries to force for bloom around Thanksgiving or Christmas. No soil needed. Fill container with stones, set in cool, dark closet for 10 days to 2 weeks. Add water when necessary. When foliage grows to 4 or 5 inches, put in warm light, and flowers will develop.	Force paperwhites at different times to have flowers blooming during several weeks.	Cut ½ inch off bottom of stem and plunge into a deep container of cool water. Allow to remain for at least one hour, longer if possible.

Bulbs, Corms, and Tubers *(Continued)*

COMMON NAME	HORTICULTURAL	ZONE(S)	HEIGHT	COLOR	WHEN IT BLOOMS	WHERE TO FIND IT
Orchid	*Vanda hybrida*	Hawaii	3 ft.	Blue, yellow, white, rose, purple	All year florist	Orchid nursery, florist
Ranunculus	*R. asiaticus* Tecolate hybrids	7–10	15–20	Yellow, orange, pink, rose, red white	May–June	Bulb company, florist
Scilla Wood-Hyacinth	*S. campanulata*	2–7	12 in.	Pink, blue, white	April–May	Bulb company, nursery, florist
Squill	*S. sibirica*	2–7	4–6 in.	Blue	March–April	Nursery, florist, bulb company
Spring Crocus	*Crocus vernus*	2–7	3–5 in.	White, purple, blue, yellow, striped	March–April	Nursery, florist, bulb company
Tulip	*Tulipa* species	3–9	6–12 in.	All colors, bicolors	March–April	Florist, bulb company
	Tulipa hybrids	3–9	8–24 in.	All colors, bicolors	March–May	Florist, bulb company
Windflower	*Anemone coronaria* 'DeCaen' and 'St. Brigid'	7–10	12 in.	Blue, scarlet, purple, rose, pink	May–June	Bulb company, florist

CULTURE	WHEN TO CUT OR BUY	HOW TO CONDITION
Grows on trees in Hawaii. Can be grown in greenhouse from baskets. Special compost of lime sphagnum moss.	Buy whenever available at florist.	Long-lasting in corsage or on long branches for decoration. Soak in water before arranging.
Grows from a small corm. Not hardy north of Washington, D.C. Often forced in greenhouse. If planted outdoors, give winter-protective mulch.	Buy in spring and summer from florist. If in own garden, cut when in full bloom.	Let stalks sit in cool water one hour before arranging. Can be wired to dry in Flower-Dri.
Plant in September and October, 5 inches deep, in rich, sandy soil. Sun or part shade. Does not force well. Let foliage dry to feed bulb for next spring.	Florist doesn't carry pots of these. Cut when in full bloom.	Let stand in cool water before arranging.
Plant in September and October, 3–4 inches deep. Plant in masses, at least 5 or 7 together. Will grow in shade, even under shrubs or as border. Let foliage dry to feed bulbs for next spring.	Does not force well. Cut when in full bloom.	Tie 5 or 10 flowers together with tape or twist'ems. Let sit in cool water in refrigerator, then arrange.
Plant in September or November, about 4 inches deep. Takes full sun or part shade. Do not cut foliage, but let it dry to feed corm for next spring.	Crocus can be forced by you or florist. Cut blossoms when in full bloom.	Let stand in cool water before arranging.
Species tulips come early, have wonderful color and shape. Some have striped, brilliant foliage. Look for them in catalogs to see size, color, and time of bloom. Good for terrace, rock garden, edge of borders.	Cut when bloom is almost open. Florists often have these in forcing pots if not in cut flowers.	Cut ½ inch off bottom of stem and plunge into a deep container of cool water. Allow to remain for at least one hour, longer if possible.
Tulip hybrids change every year. You will get to know about 12 divisions of them by studying catalogs. Some come early, some medium, some late. If you plant them, you can have blooms for 3 months. The same timing will give you forcing tulips blooming indoors from January to April. Ideal for planting outdoors is light, fertile, well-drained soil. Tulips cannot compete with shrubs or tree roots. They like sun, but will take a few hours of shade a day. Plant bulbs in late September or early October. Plant them about 10 inches deep, about 6 inches apart. When bloom is gone, cut down stem, but not foliage. Let it stand to strengthen bulb for next year's bloom. Good bulbs will bloom for 5 or 6 years.	Buy at florist from February to April. Cut when bloom is almost open. Do not cut all leaves from plant.	Condition leaves separately. Let stem stand in deep, cool water one hour before arranging. Cut stem each day and add fresh water.
Grown from tubers. Soak overnight in lukewarm water before planting. Not hardy north of Washington, D.C. Often grown by florists.	Buy in winter, spring, and summer from florist. If in own garden, cut before in full bloom.	Let stalks sit in cool water one hour before arranging. Long-lasting. Can be wired to dry in Flower-Dri.

Vines

Common Name	Horticultural	Zone(s)	Height	Color of Foliage	Blooms or Fruits	Where to Find It
Bittersweet	*Celastrus scandens*	2–6	20–40 ft.	Green	Flower insignificant; yellow-orange fruits in fall	Nursery, florist, supermarket
Boston Ivy	*Parthenocissus tricuspidata*	3–8	40 ft.	Green, turns red in autumn	Insignificant; bears pea-sized seed	Nursery
Bougainvillea	*B. glabra*	8–10	20 ft.	Green	Long season; purple, salmon, lavender, scarlet, white flower	Nursery, florist
Clematis	*C.* hybrids	3–7	10 ft.	Green	June till frost; white, pink, blue, purple, mauve, red flower	Nursery, specialty house
	C. paniculata	3–7	10–20 ft.	Green	September; small white fragrant flower	Nursery
Confederate Jasmine	*Trachelospermum jasminoides*	6–8	20 ft.	Green	April–May; white starlike flower	Nursery, florist
English Ivy	*Hedera helix*	5–8	50 ft. or ground cover	Green	Insignificant	Nursery
Honeysuckle	*Lonicera fragrantissima*	5–7	8–10 ft.	Green	January–March; fragrant white flower	Nursery
Madagascar Jasmine	*Stephanotis floribunda*	7–9	10–15 ft.	Green	All summer; fragrant white flower	Nursery
Mistletoe	*Phoradendron flavescens*	6–9	Parasite on top of trees, oaks, pecans, etc.	Yellowish green	October–December; whitish gray berries	Florist, supermarkets
Nasturtium	*Tropaeolum majus*	3–8	Climbing	Green	June till frost; scarlet to yellow flower	Seed company
	Tropaeolum hybrids	3–8	6–15 in.	Green	June till frost; scarlet to yellow flower	Seed company
Poet's Jasmine	*Jasminum officinale grandiflorum*	7–9	30 ft.	Green	All summer; fragrant white flower	Nursery

CULTURE	WHEN TO CUT OR BUY	HOW TO CONDITION
Native vine, but protected by most States from cutting. Always plant male and female shrubs near each other to guarantee berries. Sun or shade.	Buy when available at florist or supermarket. Cut your own before yellow berries split open.	Put into water to make vine pliable so you can shape it the way you wish. After that, it does not need water. Lasts all winter.
Grows in almost any soil. Takes heat and cold. Climbs stone, cement, or brick quickly and sturdily. Beautiful color change in autumn.	Cut as needed.	Last a week or 10 days, but not as long as English ivy.
Evergreen. Will not take frost. Rich soil and feeding gives best color. Likes full sun. Can be pruned to any shape or restrained.	Buy from florist when available. Cut from own vine when it is in bloom.	Strip off thorns. Split woody stem crosswise. Lasts long time in arrangement.
Prefers neutral soil. Good drainage necessary. Sandy soil better than heavy clay. Plant in fall or spring. Sun or light shade. Needs support to climb.	Cut just before petals are ready to unfold. Cut some old wood with each spray.	Take off lower leaves of vine and crush the stem to make sure the water will go into the flower. Put a tablespoon of alcohol into cool water and let the vine stay in it for at least one day or overnight. It will last one week. Easy to dry.
Fast-growing, vigorous. Can be pruned to shape. Will cover walls, columns, trellis.	Cut in fall when it blooms. Cut branches whenever they are in bloom.	Same as *C. hybrida*.
Evergreen. High-climbing. Full sun or partial shade. Won't take frost. Wonderful fragrance. Requires good support and should be trained on wire.	Buy in pots from florist. Cut when in bloom.	Take off lower leaves. Let sit in cool water one hour before arranging.
Evergreen; glossy green leaves. Will grow as ground cover or climb brick or cement walls or trees. Does best when grown on north or east side. Can suffer from sunburn in winter.	Can be purchased in a pot at florist. Cut it will last a long time.	Wash ivy, then condition it by submerging stem and leaves in cool water for half an hour. It will root if left in water. Can also be pressed or glycerinized in water.
Evergreen in mild climate. Likes sun, rich soil. Easy to grow. Very fragrant.	Cut branches when about half the flowers are in bloom.	Pull off the lower foliage of the vine and put it into cool water for at least one hour. It and the flowers should last almost a week.
Full sun, ordinary soil. Evergreen. Will not stand frost. Train to trellis or against wall where it can be seen.	Buy from florist for special occasions. Cut from vine whenever it is in bloom.	Peel off lower leaves. Place in cool water one hour, then arrange.
Grows by forcing its roots into the topmost branches of trees and lives from the sap. Used to be shot down from trees by beady-eyed farmers.	Can be bought at Christmas time.	Doesn't need conditioning.
Sow seeds in poor soil; too much fertilizer gives more leaves than flowers. Wire on trellis for climbing variety. Pick off dead flowers to keep others blooming.	Cut when in bloom.	Condition leaves separately. Tie 8 or 10 blossoms together with floral tape. Let set in cool water or refrigerate for one hour before arranging. Use in bunches for best effect.
Same as *T. majus*.	Same as *T. majus*.	Same as *T. majus*.
Sunny exposure, rich loamy soil. Will not stand frost. Semi-evergreen.	Cut when in bloom.	Pull off lower leaves. Place in cool water one hour, then arrange.

Vines (Continued)

COMMON NAME	HORTICULTURAL	ZONE(S)	HEIGHT	COLOR OF FOLIAGE	BLOOMS OR FRUITS	WHERE TO FIND IT
Smilax	*Asparagus asparagoides*	9	6–10 ft.	Green	Insignificant	Nursery, florist
Winter Creeper	*Euonymus radicans*	2–8	30 ft.	Glossy green	Autumn–winter; red berries	Nursery
Wisteria	*W. sinensis*	3–8	15–18 ft.	Green	May–June; bluish violet, white flower	Nursery

Trees and Shrubs With Decorative Foliage

American Arborvitae	*Thuja occidentalis*	2	Tree, 30–60 ft. in the wild; shrub, 10–20 ft.	Green, scalelike	Insignificant	Nursery, florist for branches
Atlas Cedar	*Cedrus atlantica glauca*	6–8	125 ft.	Blue-green needle	Flowers insignificant but has beautiful cones	Nursery, florist
Barberry Green Leaf	*Berberis thunbergii*	3–9	4–6 ft.	Green, scarlet in fall	Fall; red berries	Nursery
Red Leaf	*B. thunbergii atropurpurea*	3–9	3–5 ft.	Red	Fall; red berries	Nursery
Beech, Green, American	*Fagus grandifolia*	4 southward	100 ft.	Green		Nursery
Beech, Copper, European	*F. sylvatica cuprea*	4 southward	100 ft.	Bright copper or rosy leaves	Insignificant	Nursery
Boxwood	*Buxus sempervirens suffruticosa*	6–7	3–8 ft.	Green	Insignificant	Nursery, florist
Croton	*Codiaeum variegatum pictum*	9–10	4–5 ft.	Red, green, white, speckled, banded, curled	Insignificant	Tropical nursery, florist
Fern, Button	*Pellaea rotundifolia*	*See* Hanging Plants chart				
Flowering Crab-apple	*Malus floribunda*	3–5	30 ft.	Green	May; carmine pink flower	Nursery, florist
Holly American	*Ilex opaca*	4–6	8–30 ft.	Green	Red berries; flower insignificant	Nursery, florist

CULTURE	WHEN TO CUT OR BUY	HOW TO CONDITION
Outdoors in warm climates. Rich soil. Lots of moisture. Grown by florists to sell for decorating weddings, holidays.	Order from florist; cut outdoors when in blossom.	Keep cool in water until needed.
Extremely hardy. Evergreen. Plant fall or spring. Easy to grow. Will cling to brick or stucco walls.	Cut any time.	Clean leaves. Split stem crosswise. Long-lasting.
Sunny place, with stout support for it to climb on. Must be tied for first 2 or 3 years, then must be pruned sternly in July and September to keep it under control.	Cut when in bloom.	Peel bark on vine and let sit in cool water before arranging.
Hardy evergreen. Will take any temperature, but needs moist soil. Will not grow in prairie states.	Any time.	Evergreen, so may need to be washed in soapy water, then rinsed. Remove any dark leaves, and thin out if it looks too full. Peel bark up; cut stem 2 or 3 times. Put into deep, cool water for a night before arrangement.
Hardy evergreen with beautiful starlike clusters of needles. Any soil that is not too moist.	Florist often has branches for house decoration. You can cut some from your own tree.	Peel back bark. Cut crosswise. Will last weeks in arrangement.
Easy to grow. Not evergreen. Berries last most of winter.	Cut branches with red berries for decoration.	Let it set in ice water one hour before arranging. Can be cut during mid-March to force leaves in house before spring.
Same as Green-Leaf Barberry.	Same as Green-Leaf Barberry.	Same as Green-Leaf Barberry.
Hardy. Tolerant of any soil, if well drained.	Cut branches spring or fall for arrangements.	Can be glycerinized.
Hardy. Tolerant of any soil.	Same as Green Beech.	Same as Green Beech.
Faintly notched, rounded evergreen leaves. Grows slowly. Shallow roots. Pleasantly fragrant. Grows to perfection in Maryland, Virginia, and the Carolinas.	Any time it can be found. Cut it sparingly.	Evergreen. Same as Arborvitae. Can be preserved in glycerine.
Evergreen. Must have hot weather. No special soil or care, but rich ground and moisture give color and health to shrub. Florists raise crotons for house plants and sell leaves for arrangements.	Buy from florist when available.	Let leaves sit in cool water in refrigerator one hour before arranging. Lasts long time.
Deep, well-drained loamy soil. Fertilize regularly.	Cut blossoming branch for decoration. Cut branch of foliage early spring or fall for preserving.	Peel bark up 2 inches. Cross-cut branch. Let stand in deep water one hour before arranging. Foliage can be glycerinized.
Evergreen. Sandy loam, somewhat acid. Sun or partial shade. Need plants of both sexes to produce berries. Single berries.	Cut often when berries are red at Christmas time. Lasts weeks.	Evergreen. Keep out of cold drafts. Wipe leaves clean if needed. Split stem ½ inch, put in cool water to be refreshed, then arrange it.

133

Trees and Shrubs With Decorative Foliage *(Continued)*

COMMON NAME	HORTICULTURAL	ZONE(S)	HEIGHT	COLOR OF FOLIAGE	BLOOMS OR FRUITS	WHERE TO FIND IT
Holly English	*Ilex aquifolium*	5–6	Tree, 30–50 ft.; shrub, 3–4 ft.	Green or variegated with yellow or cream	Red berries; flower insignificant	Nursery, florist
Huckleberry, Black	*Gaylussacia baccata*	1–2	3 ft.	Green	Black shiny fruit; flower insignificant	Florist
Japanese Maple	*Acer palmatun*	3–8	10–25 ft.	Red, yellow, green combinations	Insignificant	Nursery
Juniper	*J. communis*	2 southward	6–12 ft.	Green	Flower insignificant; small dry berrylike fruit, Bluish black.	Nursery, florist
	J. virginiana	2 southward	40 ft.	Green	Tropics all year; Pea-sized bluish fruit	Nursery, florist
Magnolia, Bull Bay	*M. grandiflora*	5 southward	60–100 ft.	Green	June–July; large fragrant white flower	Nursery, florist
Mountain Laurel	*Kalmia latifolia*	3–4	Shrub, 4–10 ft.; tree, No. Carolina Mts.	Green	May–June; pink or whitish clusters	Nursery, florist, wild
Palm Fan-Leaved Washington Palm	*Washingtonia*	8–9	60 ft.	Grayish green	Insignificant	Nursery, tropical
Chinese Fan	*Livistona chinensis*	8–9	4–6 ft. in pot	Green	Insignificant	Nursery, tropical
Feather-Leaved Kentia Palm	*Howeia fosteriana*	8–9	12 in.–6 ft. in pot	Green	Insignificant	Nursery, florist
Cane Palm	*Chrysalidocarpus lutescens*	8–9	5 ft. in pot	Olive green	Insignificant	Nursery, florist
Lady Palm	*Rhapis excelsa*	8–9	5–6 ft. in pot	Green	Insignificant	Nursery, florist
Pear	*Pyrus communis*	4–6	25 ft.	Green	April; white flower	Nursery, friend
Pin Oak	*Quercus palustris*	4–7	80–90 ft.	Green	Insignificant; has acorns	Nursery, friend
Pittosporum	*P. tobira*	7–8	6–15 ft.	Green or green edged with cream	June–July; fragrant white to rose pink flower	Nursery, florist, friend
Purple-Leaf Plum	*Prunus cerasifera pissardii*	3–5	15–25 ft.	Purple	April–May; large pink flower	Nursery, friend

CULTURE	WHEN TO CUT OR BUY	HOW TO CONDITION
More difficult to grow than American holly; not so hardy. Spiny teeth on leaves. Berries in clusters. Need plants of both sexes to produce them. Does not like dry, hot summers.	Same as American Holly.	Same as American Holly.
Shade; dry, sandy soil. Hardy.	Any time from florist.	Not evergreen. Split stem. Put into cool water.
Slow-growing small tree planted for its colorful foliage. Easily grown in any soil.	Branches cut in fall for beautiful color.	Peel bark up 2 inches. Cut stem crosswise. Let sit in cool water before arranging. Can be forced in early March for spring decoration.
Evergreen. Easy to grow. Light sandy soil. Will stand dry wind. Leaves needlelike, spreading.	Any time.	Wipe leaves clean if necessary. Peel up bark. Cross-cut. Put in cool water. Keeps weeks or months. Can be glycinerized.
Same as *J. communis.*	Same as *J. communis.*	Same as *J. communis.*
Evergreen. Oblong leaves alternate; 5–8 inches long, shiny green above, rusty wooly beneath. Hardy in south. Foliage dense. Evergreen.	Whenever it can be bought.	Cut branch on slant. Peel bark up 2 or 3 inches. Cut stem crosswise. Put into cool water. Keeps for weeks. Foliage can be glycerinized and lasts forever.
Native eastern North American broad-leaf evergreen shrub. Leaves supple, without marginal teeth, narrowly oval, 2–4 inches, tough, leathery. Partly shade, acid soil.	With blossoms, May or June. Any time for foliage.	Cut branch on slant. Peel back bark. Cross-cut stem. Put into cool water. Evergreen, long-lasting. Foliage can be glycerinized.
Fan-leaved palm: Native to California. Evergreen. Ringed trunk, crown of fan-like leaves which are divided into narrow fingers.	Take leaves whenever you can.	Not used in arrangements.
Feather-leaved palm: Outdoors in Southern California and Florida. Sometimes in tubs. Evergreen, ringed, spineless trunk. *See* Potted Plants.	Same as Fan-leaved Palm.	Not used in arrangements.
Well-drained, rich clay soil. Full sun.	Cut blossoming branch for decoration. Cut foliage branch for preserving either in early spring or fall.	Peel bark 2 inches up. Cross-cut branch. Let stand in deep water one hour before arranging. Foliage can be glycerinized.
Tolerates any soil that is not wet or alkaline.	Cut branch in fall to preserve.	Not used in arrangements.
Large, evergreen. Used in South and Pacific Coast. Foliage dark green, leathery, thick. Needs rich garden loam. Sunny, partial shade. Often grown as pot plant.	Cut any time. Buy from florist any time.	Wipe leaves if dusty. Cut on slant, peel up bark, cross-cut stems. Put into cool water; lasts long time.
Ordinary garden soil. Ornamental tree.	Cut in early spring when foliage is purple, to preserve it.	Use glycerine and water.

135

Trees and Shrubs With Decorative Foliage *(Continued)*

COMMON NAME	HORTICULTURAL	ZONE(S)	HEIGHT	COLOR OF FOLIAGE	BLOOMS OR FRUITS	WHERE TO FIND IT
Pussy Willow	*Salix discolor*	2–8	8–10 ft.	Green	March–April; green and yellow catkins	Nursery, florist
Red Maple	*Acer rubrum*	2–8	75–120 ft.	Green	Tiny red flowers before leaves unfold	Nursery
Rhododendron	*R. maximum*	4	10 ft.	Green	June–July; white to rose pink flower	Nursery, florist, friend
Silver Dollar	*Eucalyptus polyanthemos*	9–10	30 ft.	Blue-green	Insignificant	Nursery, florist
Tulip	*Liriodendron tulipifera*	4–8	120 ft.	Green or Bluish green	May–June; large white flower with orange band	Nursery
White Pine	*Pinus strobus*	2–8	90–150 ft.	Blue-green needles	Insignificant; has pine cones	Nursery
Winged Euonymus	*Euonymus alatus*	3–8	6–9 ft.	Pale green in spring; brilliant rosy red in fall.	October–November; red fruit	Nursery
Yew Japanese	*Taxus cuspidata* *Taxus cuspidata nana*	2–8 3–8	20 ft. 4–6 ft.	Green Green	Winter; red fruit Winter; red fruit	Nursery, florist Nursery, florist
English	*Taxus baccata*	6–8	4–20 ft.	Green	Winter; red fruit	Nursery, florist

Trees and Shrubs With Blossoms in Season

Acacia	*Acacia*	9	15 ft.	Green to bluish green	Spring; golden yellow flower	Nursery, florist
Azalea Rhododendron	*R.* Exbury hybrids	4 south-ward	3–4 ft.	Green	May–June; vivid yellow, salmon, red orange, white, pink, some blotched	Nursery, florist, friend
	R. kaempferi	5 south-ward	5–9 ft.	Green	May–June; salmon pink flower	Nursery, florist, friend
	R. Kurume hybrids	5 south-ward	3 ft.	Green	April–May; flowers white pink, coral, salmon, red	Nursery, florist

CULTURE	WHEN TO CUT OR BUY	HOW TO CONDITION
Tolerates all soils, even moist and wet places. Hardy.	Buy in spring. Cut in January or February to place in house. Can be cut when catkins are out and kept all spring.	Put in water to make branch pliable to desired shape. After that, no water necessary or catkins will turn into leaves.
Native tree, easily grown. Will grow in moist places as well as in ordinary garden soil.	Branch is beautiful in fall to cut for decorating house.	Peel back bark 2 inches. Cut stem crosswise and soak in cool water before arranging.
Broad-leafed evergreen. Native of eastern North America. Very hardy; dense growth; will take shade. Large leaf; large center blossoms. Good light, no direct sun. Acid soil, rich in humus. Protect from wind. Don't cultivate; put on mulch. Protect in winter with deep layer of oak leaves.	Cut blossoms in June or July. Cut branches for arrangement any time.	Wipe off leaves, cut stems on slant, peel up bark, cross-cut stem. Put into cool water. Foliage can be glycerinized. Long-lasting.
Evergreen. Will stand cool temperatures but not frost. Full sun. Any kind of soil. Does well in California climate.	Buy stems of foliage from florist all year. In climate where it grows, cut branches any time.	Excellent foliage with any flowers. Can be hung to dry or preserved in glycerine and water.
Native tree of eastern North America; stately. Only spring planting for growing trees. Deep rich moist soil. Needs much space around it.	Cut branches with flowers in bloom.	Peel back bark 2 inches. Cut stem crosswise. Let stand in water one hour before arranging. Can be forced in early February in the house.
Evergreen with blue-green needle leaves, 5 in each cluster. Stately. Fairly tolerant of heat, dryness.	Branches can be cut in fall or winter for decoration.	Peel back bark. Cut end of branch crosswise. Lasts weeks in arrangement.
Any good soil. Sun or part shade; likes good drainage. Bark of branches have unusual corky-winged edges. This plus its late lasting color makes it very decorative.	Cut in spring or fall for effective arrangements.	Split woody branch to let it absorb water for one hour before arranging.
Hardy evergreen. Narrow leaves with sharp tips. Will live anywhere, but thrives in cool, moist sites.	Summer or winter.	Clean if needed. Cut on slant. Peel up bark. Cross-cut stem and put into cool water. Lasts months.
Evergreen. Not very hardy. Needs cool moisture. Won't stand harsh winds. Variety *T. baccata repandens* is low, much hardier than the species.	Same as Japanese Yew.	Same as Japanese Yew.
Evergreen trees grow in California, but best acacia is flown from Southern France in spring.	Buy in spring from florist.	Condition in cool water before arranging. Can be preserved by letting water evaporate from bowl until flowers dry. Color remains true.
Not evergreen. Hardy big blooms. Shipped fall or spring. Results of years of experiments in England. Will take colder temperatures than any other deciduous azalea.	Cut for arrangement or buy when 3 or 4 flowers are open on each stem or cluster. Buds open well in water.	Peel bark up about an inch. Split with a sharp knife about an inch up the stem. Put into deep, cool water for at least one hour, longer if possible, before arrangement is made.
Showy flowers. Hardy. Not evergreen.	Same as *R.* Exbury.	Same as *R.* Exbury.
Evergreen or in cold climates more or less deciduous. Low, compact.	Same as *R.* Exbury.	Evergreen foliage can be glycerinized.

Trees and Shrubs With Blossoms in Season *(Continued)*

COMMON NAME	HORTICULTURAL	ZONE(S)	HEIGHT	COLOR	WHEN IT BLOOMS	WHERE TO FIND IT
Azalea Rhododendron *(Continued)*	*R. Mollis* hybrids	4–5	3–6 ft.	Green	May–June; yellow, orange, or reddish flower	Nursery, florist, friend
Beauty Bush	*Kolkwitzia amabilis*	3–6	4–6 ft.	Green	May or June; profuse terminal clusters of pink bell-shaped flowers	Nursery, florist, friend
Bird-of-Paradise	*Strelitzia reginae*	9–10	3 ft.	Dark green	All year in tropical zone; flowers orange-red with blue tongues	Florist, nursery
Bridal Wreath	*Spiraea vanhouttei*	3 southward	4–6 ft.	Green	May–June; white flower	Nursery, friend. supermarket
Butterfly Bush	*Buddleia davidii*	5–6 southward	4–10 ft.	Green with whitish underside	Mid-July till frost; flowers lilac, purple, red, white, with orange spot at throat; nodded spike, 5–12 in. long	Nursery, friend
Camellia	*C. japonica*	Middle of 5–7	6–15 ft.	Green	October–March; pink, red, white, variegated flowers	Nursery, florist, friend
	C. sasanqua	5–8	4–7 ft.	Green	October–December; rose, pink, white flowers	Nursery, florist, friend
Dogwood	*Cornus florida*	4–7	20–30 ft.	Green becoming purplish red in fall	April–June; white or pink flower, red fruit	Nursery, florist, friend
Flowering Crabapple	*Malus floribunda*	3–8	15–25 ft.	Green	May; white, pink, rose flowers	Nursery
Forsythia	*F. intermedia* var. *spectabilis*	5–7	7–9 ft.	Green	April–May; golden yellow flowers in clusters	Nursery, florist, friend
Heath	*Erica*	5–6	8–12 in.	Green or bronze	March–May; red, pink, white flowers	Nursery, greenhouse

CULTURE	WHEN TO CUT OR BUY	HOW TO CONDITION
Not evergreen. Erect shrub. Shallow rooted. Sandy, acid soil. Filtered light. Don't cultivate. Three-inch mulch of oak leaves or pine needles.	Same as *R.* Exbury.	Same as *R.* Exbury.
Easy to grow. Full sun. Grows three-quarters as wide as it is high. Branches hang in bloom like pink waterfall.	Cut when blossom is open.	Same as all woody-stemmed branches.
Tropical evergreen shrub from South Africa. Grows outdoors in Florida, southern California. Full sun all year. Plenty of water in summer months. House plants take long time to bloom.	Buy house plant and order stalk from florist. If shown outdoors, cut when in bloom.	Let stalks sit in cool water before arranging. Lasts long time.
Very hardy, beautiful. Stands city dirt and smoke better than most shrubs. Will grow in any soil. Likes moist site. Arching branches; leaves green, faintly three-veined, often red or orange in autumn.	Cut for arranging when a quarter to a half of branch is open.	Split upward for an inch, and crosswise. Put into cool water in shady room for at least one hour before arranging. Lasts about a week.
Easy in any garden soil, if in warm enough zone. Full sun. Rich soil. Leaves simple, 6–9 inches long. Finely toothed.	Cut when in bloom. Lasts long.	Split upward for an inch, and crosswise. Put into cool water in shady room for at least one hour before arranging.
Evergreen. Plant bushy. Leaves are finely toothed, 3 to 4 inches long. Flowers waxy, double in some varieties. Well-drained moist soil, quite acid. Does better if protected from early morning sun. Spray foliage to increase humidity. Mulch with peat moss or pine needles.	Cut for arranging when blossoms are open.	Same as Butterfly Bush.
Evergreen. Same soil as *C. japonica,* but will tolerate more sun and more cold. Leaves 1 to 2½ inches long. Blossoms open smaller than *C. japonica;* have perfume. Easily branched. Decorative for landscape planting.	Same as *C. japonica.*	Same as Butterfly Bush.
Native tree of eastern North America. Partial shade, not much wind. Leaves oval, 3 to 5 inches long, pointed at tips. Not easy to transplant.	Symbol of spring! In bloom.	Peel bark 2 inches from end of branch. Cut crosswise, then let soak in deep, cool water one hour before arranging. Can be forced in midwinter for early spring flowering.
Easily grown. Very hardy. Plant in spring in deep hole. Stake first year.	Cut branch when blossoms are almost open.	Peel back bark 2 inches. Cut branch crosswise. Set in cool water one hour before arranging. Can be forced in early March for spring flowering.
Any soil. Full sun. Blooms before leaves appear. Graceful, arching branches. Prune several old stalks right after blooming to allow new growth to start.	When bloom begins. Can be forced by cutting in February and bringing indoors.	Split upward for an inch, and cut crosswise. Put into cool water in shady room for at least one hour before arranging.
Likes sun, sandy and acid soil. Evergreen. Best planted in masses or in rock gardens. Also good as potted plant.	Greenhouses offer heath as potted plant. Not very good as cut flowers, but dries naturally and easily.	A shrub. The stems must be stripped of leaves and cut crosswise to take water.

Trees and Shrubs With Blossoms in Season *(Continued)*

COMMON NAME	HORTICULTURAL	ZONE(S)	HEIGHT	COLOR	WHEN IT BLOOMS	WHERE TO FIND IT
Heather	*Calluna vulgaris*	5–6	8–15 in.	Green or bronze	July–October; white, pink, red, purple flowers	Nursery, greenhouse
Hibiscus	*H. rosa-sinensis*	8–9	6–20 ft.	Green	All year in tropics; pink, coral, red, white, yellow flowers	Nursery, florist
Hydrangea	*H. macrophylla* 'Hortensia'	4–7	3–4 ft.	Green	July–September; pink, blue, white flowers	Nursery, florist
	H. paniculata grandiflora 'Peegee'	2–5	8–25 ft.	Green	Summer–fall; flowers white fading to pink	Nursery, florist
Lantana	*L. camara*	8–10	Shrub, 3–5 ft.; bedding plant, 18–30 in.	Green July till frost;	All year, tropical; July till frost; flowers yellow, orange, red, often at same time	Nursery, florist
Lilac	*Syringa vulgaris*	3–7	10–20 ft.	Green	Spring; lilac, purple, white flowers	Nursery, supermarket, florist
Lilac, French	*Syringa* hybrids	3–7	10–20 ft.	Green	Spring; flowers white, lilac, purple, blue, pink, reddish	Nursery, supermarket, florist
Mock Orange	*Philadelphus virginalis*	2–6	4–6 ft.	Green	June; flowers white, double in clusters	Nursery, florist
	Philadelphus coronarius	2–6	6–10 ft.	Green	June; flowers white, single in clusters	Nursery, florist
Oleander	*Nerium oleander*	6–10	Shrub, 8–25 ft; 4–6 ft. in tub	Green	April–October as a shrub, June–August, in tub; flowers red, coral, pink, white	Nursery, florist
Poinsettia	*Euphorbia pulcherrima*	8–10	6–10 ft. or shrub in pot	Green	Several weeks in tropics, insignificant flowers with red, pink, white bracts.	Nursery, florist

CULTURE	WHEN TO CUT OR BUY	HOW TO CONDITION
Evergreen sub-shrub. Sandy, acid soil. Has become naturalized in Nantucket and Martha's Vineyard. Does well in sandy slopes.	Cut stalks when in bloom. They dry without any trouble.	Can be kept in water until bloom dies or can be dried without trouble by hanging, head down, in airy spot.
Well-known evergreen tropical shrub. Grows in full sun. Takes dry weather, but improves with moisture and feeding. Makes fine potted plant.	Blooms constantly in tropics. Flower usually lasts only one day.	No need to put in water. Use on long bamboo stem or lay on table.
Shrub. Leaves 3–6 inches long. Coarsely toothed. Globe-shaped clusters of blossoms. Easy to grow in sun or shade.	Cut when in bloom. Florists force this as potted plant. Blossoms huge. Can be left till almost dry, then cut to hang until dry.	Split upward for an inch, and cut crosswise. Put into cool water in shady room for at least one hour before arranging. Smaller blooms can be dried upside down in Flower-Dri.
Leaves oval, rounded at base, 3–5 inches long and toothed on margin. Can be grown in tree form. Grows well in city or windswept garden.	Cut when in bloom. Blossoms will dry on shrub or can be dried in house.	Same as *H. macrophylla*.
Evergreen. Set plants in full sun in rather poor soil. Vigorous. Takes heat and sun. Blooms constantly in tropical climate. Not hardy where there is frost. Can be grown in pot and kept inside in cold climate.	Cut when in bloom. Pots are available at florist.	Condition like all woody branches.
Easy to grow in any soil. Widely spreading. Sometimes treelike leaves, 2–6 inches long, heart-shaped to oval. Flowers fragrant. Don't fertilize more than every 2 years, otherwise bloom is lost to leaves. Remove withered blossoms and seed pods to make better bloom next year. Remove suckers. Lilacs like to have rich soil, sunlight, and moisture.	Whenever bloom is ready. Cut long branches for decoration. This helps to prune shrub.	Many methods of conditioning. Remove leaves near blossoms so bloom shows. Peel bark up 2 inches. Cut stem crosswise. Put complete branch, blossom, and stem in deep, cool water in washtubs. Leave overnight; next day arrange. Will keep a week.
Hybrid of common lilac. Some single, some double. Exquisite colors and shapes. Sometimes without fragrance. Rich soil.	Same as Lilac.	Same as Lilac.
Hybrid. Brown, peeling bark or grayish and only slightly peeling. Leaves 2–3 inches long, ovalish. Extremely fragrant. Easy to grow. Tolerates all kinds of soil.	Cut when in bloom in June. Fragrance adds to beauty of flowers.	Take off leaves at base of stem. Peel bark up 2–3 inches. Split crosswise. Put in deep water to condition one hour before arranging.
Tall, single blossoms. Widely cultivated. Sometimes too fragrant.	Same as *P. virginalis*.	Same as *P. virginalis*.
Evergreen. Any good garden soil. Full sun. Can stand smoke, dust, salt spray. In pot in cold climates must be wintered in cool sunroom or basement.	Dangerous to use as decoration, for leaves, flowers, and juice are poisonous if eaten.	Use shrubs in pots for decoration.
In zones where it grows outdoors like a shrub, it blooms fall and winter. In greenhouse it sets color in its bracts when the days become short. No electric light at night.	Buy from florist when in full color. New hybrids will last for months. Outside they can be cut whenever you want them.	Stem has milky liquid that will run out. Sear end with candle flame before putting into water. When you take stem out to change water, cut stem and sear again. Can be forced in February for early budding.

141

Trees and Shrubs With Blossoms in Season *(Continued)*

COMMON NAME	HORTICULTURAL	ZONE(S)	HEIGHT	COLOR	WHEN IT BLOOMS	WHERE TO FIND IT
Pussy Willow	*Salix discolor*	3–7	10–18 ft. shrub or tree	Green	March–April; gray catkins, yellow when fully open	Nursery, super-market, florist
Redbud	*Cercis canadensis*	4–7	Tree, 7–30 ft.; sometimes shrubby, 15 ft.	Green	April–May; rose, pink flowers	Nursery, florist
Scarlet Firethorn	*Pyracantha coccinea lalandi*	6–10	10 ft.	Green	White flowers in spring; fall and winter, orange, scarlet fruit	Nursery
Scotch Broom	*Cytisus scoparius*	5–6	4–9 ft.	Green; stems also green	May–June; yellow flower	Nursery, greenhouse
Sour Cherry	*Prunus cerasus*	2–4	35 ft.; dwarf, 10–12 ft.	Green	May; white flower, red fruit	Nursery
Ti Leaves	*Cordyline terminalis*	10, Hawaii	8–10 ft.	Pink, white, purple, metallic, striped	Insignificant	Nursery, greenhouse
Weigela	*W. florida*	3–7	8–10 ft.	Red	May–June; pink, red bell-shaped flowers	Nursery
Winged Spindle Tree	*Euonymus alatus*	3 south-ward	6–9 ft.	Green becoming brilliant rose-crimson in fall	Insignificant	Nursery

House Plants

COMMON NAME	HORTICULTURAL	DESCRIPTION AND CULTURAL SUGGESTIONS	LIGHT	TEMPERATURE*
Aeonium	*A. arboreum*	Succulent. Desert plant. Likes sandy soil.	Sun, south window	Will take hot temperature: 65–75.
African Violet	*Saintpaulia ionantha* (many varieties)	Low-growing, rounded plant about 8–10 inches high. Not too easy, but blooms all year.	Low light. East or west window. Does well under arti-ficial light. No direct sun.	65–75 best.
Aloe	*A. variegata*	Perennial, desert plant. Sandy soil.	Full sun, south	Likes heat: 65–75.
Alyssum	*A. maritimum* (*Lobularia maritima*)	Buy potted plants in spring: white, pink, lavender. White best.	Full sun in window 4 hours daily.	Warm: 68–72. Cooler at night.

(*Degrees Fahrenheit)

CULTURE	WHEN TO CUT OR BUY	HOW TO CONDITION
Tolerates moisture as well as sun. Leaves 3–4 inches long. Roots easily. Catkins are erect on female branches; come before the leaves.	Cut twigs any time after January 15, and force in house. Or buy from florist in February or March.	Cut end of twig crosswise; put into water to soften so it can be bent to desired shape. After that, no water is necessary. Use many branches together rather than singly.
An undergrowth tree native to Kentucky, Maryland, and southward. Does well in half shady place. Rich, humus soil. Flowers appear before leaves on bare twigs. Very showy.	Whenever in bloom.	Condition like all woody branches.
Evergreen shrub; thorny. Open sun, well drained soil. Can be single treelike shrub trained against wall or hedge.	Cut from own shrub when berries are developed.	Cut stalk crosswise. Take off lower foliage and set in cool water an hour before arranging.
Grows in any soil, though prefers some lime on it.	Greenhouse can usually provide branches from spring through fall. Cut when in bloom.	Good for foliage in dried arrangement. Easily molded to curve or shape as wanted. Dries easily by hanging head down.
Likes fairly heavy soil but good drainage. Plant in spring with large hole and 20 feet on each side for growth. Does not need pruning. Spray to prevent insect and rust.	If you can spare a branch of blossoms, cut when they are almost open.	Peel bark 2 inches from end of branch. Cut crosswise, then let soak in deep, cool water one hour before arranging.
Grows in Hawaii and southern Florida and California. For house plants and terrace plants, go to florist or nursery.	Buy from florist when you can order them. Cut from shrub when you want them.	Can be kept in water or glycerinized.
Very hardy. Easy to grow. Sun. Prune after flowering.	Cut branches in full bloom.	Take off lower leaves. Peel bark up 2 inches. Cut branch crosswise. Let stand in deep water one hour before arranging. Roots well.
Easy to grow. Takes sun. Horizontal growth. Curious corky bark or branches, gives it a winged look.	Cut in late spring after leaves are light green. Also cut in fall for wonderful rose color of leaves. Bark fascinating.	Split upward for an inch, and cut crosswise. Put into cool water in shady room for at least one hour before arranging.

HUMIDITY	WATERING	FEEDING
Likes dryness.	Once a week.	Give mild mixture of water-soluble food every 3 months.
Don't let it get really dry or really wet. Set pot on pebbles to increase humidity.	Water in morning with warm water drawn the night before. Set pot in saucer of water until soil at surface shows moisture.	Must be fed regularly with complete water-soluble fertilizer according to directions on package.
Not necessary.	Moderate. Let dry between waterings.	Feed every 6 months.
Needs humidity.	Loves moisture. Water daily.	Fertilize every month, one-half strength.

House Plants *(Continued)*

COMMON NAME	HORTICULTURAL	DESCRIPTION AND CULTURAL SUGGESTIONS	LIGHT	TEMPERATURE*
Amaryllis	*Hippeastrum* hybrids (American-grown, Holland-grown, South African-grown)	Large, tender bulb. Can be bought potted, or you can pot in 4-inch plastic pot. Bloom stalk comes before foliage. 1–2 feet tall. Second stalk follows. Huge blooms pink, red, salmon, white, striped. Will flower year after year.	Direct sunlight 4 hours daily to bring bloom. Out of sun to keep bloom lasting.	Warm: 70–75. Bottom heat forces bloom. Cooler, 65–70, after bloom.
Azalea	*Rhododendron indicum*	Rich soil, highly acid. After blooming, trim the branches back a little.	Sun, south window. Put outdoors in summer if possible.	Cool: 50–60.
Basil 'Dark Opal'	*Ocimum basilicum*	Buy plants for arrangements. Some don't like this taste in dishes.	Full sun.	Warm: 60–70.
Basil, Sweet	*Ocimum basilicum*	Buy plants for kitchen windowsill for cooking.	Full sun.	Warm: 60–70.
Begonia Fibrous Begonia 'Linda'	*B. semperflorens*	Green-leaved, deep pink, ever-blooming. 8 inches high. Pinch to keep dwarf.	Sunlight or reflected light.	Warm: 60–70.
Tuberous Begonia American Double Ruffled Double Rose Form Picotee	*B. tuberhybrida*	Buy potted plants or start tubers under growing lights. If bloom wanted for winter, buy tubers, keep in cool, dark place till August, then plant them.	4 hours' sun from November to March. Filtered sun in spring and summer.	Warm: 68–72. Cooler at night.
Bird-of-Paradise	*Strelitzia reginae*	Buy plant in pot. Leaves grow to 12–15 inches. Plant can be 2–3 feet tall. Flowers orange and blue. Sometimes takes 2–3 years to bloom. Does not like to be transplanted.	Direct sun, 4 hours a day.	Warm: 68–72. Cooler at night.
Boxwood, Dwarf English	*Buxus sempervirens suffruticosa*	Evergreen, small dark green leaf, slow growth.	Full sun or shade or no light.	Warm or cool.
Butterfly Palm or Cane Plam	*Chrysalidocarpus lutescens*	Feather-shaped foliage. Graceful.	Bright light but not sun.	Moderately warm: 65.
Calamondin Orange	*Citrus mitis*	Evergreen. Glossy green leaves, orange- colored fruit.	Sunny or bright light.	Cool: 50–60.
Calceolaria	*C. herbeohybrida*	For temporary display only. Yellow, orange, or green flowers.	Shade from direct sun.	Cool: 50–60.
Camellia	*C. japonica*	Evergreen plant. Buy potted plant. Flowers pink, red, white. Blooms September–April. Spray or mist foliage and buds. Grows to 2 feet tall.	Bright, indirect light. Filtered sun.	Warm: 65–75. Cooler at night.
Chinese Evergreen	*Aglaeonema simplex*	Evergreen foliage.	Shade or good light without strong sun.	Warm: 65—70.
Chives	*Allium schoenoprasum*	Buy 2 or 3 pots to grow on kitchen windowsill, or start seed at different times to keep it growing. Decorative; good for cooking.	Sunlight.	Warm: 65–70.

*(*Degrees Fahrenheit)*

HUMIDITY	WATERING	FEEDING
LIkes humidity.	Water thoroughly when starts to grow bulb. After spike appears, water daily, and all through blooming. After bloom, when weather is warm, set plant outside or on terrace. Water during summer until early September. Without water until leaves turn yellow. Cut leaves off, turn pot on side to rest until it shows signs of life again. Then take into light, water, and it will bloom again.	Give soluble feeding of about one-half strength every 2 weeks while bulb is growing and getting ready to bloom. When bloom is gone, feed once a month during summer.
Keep humidity high.	Water frequently.	Feed every 2 weeks with soluble fertilizer.
Likes dry soil.	Daily.	Fertilize one-half strength once a month.
Likes dry soil.	Daily.	Fertilize one-half strength once a month.
Likes sitting on damp pebbles.	Likes water, but let plant dry out between waterings.	No nitrogen, but fertilizer with large amounts of phosphate and potash once a week.
Needs humidity. Soil moist.	Barely enough water to keep soil moist.	Feed every week with one-quarter of amount recommended.
Needs humidity.	Water thoroughly, then let soil dry out between waterings.	Do not fertilize.
Likes humidity.	Water generously each day.	Fertilize every 3 months.
Soil should stay moist.	Daily.	Once a month, half strength.
Moderate humidity.	Daily or every other day.	Once or twice a month.
Moderate humidity.	Daily.	Do not fertilize.
As much as possible, set on pebbles.	Water each morning. Spray water over foliage and flower buds.	Buy special camellia fertilizer (acid kind) and feed plant early spring and early and midsummer. After bloom is gone, feed with one teaspoon ammonium sulphate to one gallon of water for a month, until new growth is seen.
Moderate humidity.	Daily or every other day.	Once a month.
Not necessary.	Water generously.	Do not fertilize.

House Plants (*Continued*)

Common Name	Horticultural	Description and Cultural Suggestions	Light	Temperature*
Christmas Cactus	*Schlumbergera bridgesii*	Deep pink flowers from November to January, bare gray cactus branches rest of the year. Special tricks needed to get bloom.	Bright sun from August to November. Filtered light during bloom and in spring. Moderate shade outdoors or on terrace till August.	Warm: 70–75 from August to November. Cool after bloom till spring: 60–70. Warm during summer. Let stay outside or on terrace until nearly frost.
Chrysanthemum	*C. hortorum* (sometimes, *C. morifolium*)	12–24 inches.	Bright sun.	Warmer by day, cool at night: 60–70.
Coleus	*C. blumei*	Many colors. Study catalogs. 6 inches to 2 feet. Roots easily.	Sunny or lightly shaded.	Warm: 65–70.
Croton	*Codiaeum variegatum*	Foliage plant. Leaves twisted, mottled, red, green, brown, yellow. Spray regularly to prevent red spider.	Full sun.	Hot: 65–80.
Cyclamen	*C. persicum*	Buy potted plant. Rose, red, pink, white. Blooms mid-autumn to mid-spring. Difficult to carry over to next year.	East window. Bright indirect light or filtered sunlight.	Cool: 65. Cooler at night.
Dracaena	*D. deremensis warneckii*	Evergreen plant from tropical Africa. A green leaf with slender white line in center and edge. Hardy. One of best foliage plants for home decoration. Takes dryness.	Strong light or partial sun, east or west window.	Warm: 65–75.
Dumbcane	*Dieffenbachia picta*	2–4 feet. Green leaves, spotted with white. No drafts.	Good light. No direct sun.	Warm: 65–70.
	D. picta 'Zebra'	Graceful plant 4 feet tall. Green leaves with yellow markings. No drafts.	Bright indirect light. No sun.	Warm: 65–70.
Dwarf Orange	*Citrus calamondin*	Beautiful bright green leaves, fragrant white blossoms, green and orange fruit. Less than 2 feet tall. Hardy.	South or west window, 4 hours sun per day.	Warm: 68–72. Cooler at night.
Echeveria	*Echeveria*	Succulent. Rosette-forming plants. Sandy soil.	Sun, south window.	Warm: 70 and higher.
'Emerald Ripple'	*Peperomia capreata*	Tiny, pleated leaves. Hardy.	Shade. No direct sun.	Warm: 65–70.
English Ivy	*Hedera helix*	Green leaves or white edged leaves. Bushy or trailing. Very decorative.	In windows with any exposure or center of room with indirect light.	Cool temperature is best: 60–65.
Fiddle-Leaf Fig	*Ficus lyrata*	Evergreen plant. Small or tree-size. Shiny green leathery leaves, 12–18 inches long, shaped like a fiddle. Hardy. Does not like dry soil.	Filtered light or sun. Even lives a while in dark places.	Any temperature.

(*Degrees Fahrenheit*)

HUMIDITY	WATERING	FEEDING
Needs humidity from August to end of bloom. Not needed from spring to fall.	Water daily and evenly while growing and blooming. After blooming, let rest and water very little. Outdoors or on terrace during summer and until August, almost no water. Begin watering again when brought in house.	Fertilize one-half strength every 2 weeks while plant is growing and blooming. No food after bloom is gone and in rest period in summer. Feed again in August when plant is taken in house.
Good drainage.	Good drainage. Not wet soil.	Once a week, mixed with water.
Moist, humusy soil.	Do not water too much. Let soil become completely dry, then set pot into saucer of water till top is wet again.	Every 4 months, half-strength feeding.
Soil moist. Set on pebble tray.	Daily. Spray leaves with warm water to keep dampness and get rid of red spider.	Fertilize every 3 months.
Needs humidity.	Water each morning. Don't get water on crown of corm.	Every 2 weeks, half strength.
Moderate to high humidity.	Water freely. Wash leaves often.	Nitrogen feeding once a month.
Needs moisture but never let soil become soggy or waterlogged.	Water heavily, then let soil dry completely before watering again.	Every 3 months, half strength.
Never let soil become soggy.	Water generously. Let soil become dry between waterings.	Feed half strength every 2–3 months.
Needs humidity.	Water generously. Let soil become dry between waterings.	Give occasional feedings in early spring, early and late summer.
Not necessary.	Water thoroughly, then let soil dry out completely before watering again.	Once every 6 months give half-strength fertilizer.
Not necessary.	Don't water too much. Let soil dry out between waterings. Put pot into saucer with water under it until top is damp.	Every 3 or 4 months give half-strength feeding.
Can grow in water as well as soil.	Requires moderate watering. Wash leaves often.	Once a month.
Keep soil moist.	If plant is in cool room, do not water much. Otherwise water generously.	No fertilizer needed.

House Plants *(Continued)*

Common Name	Horticultural	Description and Cultural Suggestions	Light	Temperature*
Flowering Maple	*Abutilon* hybrids	Maple-shaped leaf; blooms white, rose, orange, yellow.	South window.	Warm: 68–72. Cooler at night.
Geranium	*Pelargonium hortorum*	Hybrids available from florist. Red, pink, white, coral 8–15 inches. Hardy.	All geraniums: Sun and bright light.	All geraniums: Warm: 60–70. Cooler at night.
Dwarf and Miniature		3–8 inches tall. Single and double.		
Fancy Leaf		Beautiful leaves. Study catalogs.		
Scented-Leaved				
Rose Scented	*P. graveolens*	Deeply cut foliage. Lavender blooms.		
Oak Leaf	*P. quercifolium*	Pungent scent. Showy pink bloom.		
Peppermint	*P. tomentosum*	Leaves large, soft, "minty."		
Olive Scented	*P. denticulatum*	Deeply cut leaves. Pink blooms.		
Lemon Scented	*P. crispum*	Leaves small, ruffled. Blooms pink.		
Nutmeg	*P. odoratissimum*	Silvery gray, scented leaf. White blooms.		
Miscellaneous group				
Ginger		Showy lavender bloom. Sweet scent. Small round leaf.		
Rosebud Geranium	*P. hortorum*	Rose-red shading to white center.		
Apple-Blossom Rosebud		Beautiful variety.		
Hibiscus	*H. rosa-sinensis*	Evergreen shrub or tree. Blooms white, cream yellow, salmon, red.	South or west window. Sun.	Hot: 70 and higher. Cooler at night.
Hyacinth	*Hyacinthus orientalis*	Buy plant in bud or bloom. Or force in September. Don't cut off foliage until it turns yellow. Blue, white, pink, yellow. Save bulbs to plant outdoors that summer.	Sunlight, except when in bloom, then partial shade.	Warm: 68. Cooler at night.
Impatiens	*I. sultanii*	Easy annual; blooms continuously. 15 inches high. Prune to keep it bushy. Pink, red.	Indirect light or shade.	Warm: 70. Cooler at night.
Dwarf Impatiens 'Imp' Series F₁ 'Elfin' Series F₁ 'Grande' Mixed	*I. sultana nana*	Dwarf plants, 6–8 inches. Red, pink, rose, coral, orange.	Indirect light or shade.	Warm: 70. Cooler at night.
Jade Plant	*Crassula argentea*	Succulent. Can be small, 8 inches, or tree-size, 3 feet.	Any exposure. Sun, half sun, shade.	Warm: 65–70.
Jerusalem Cherry	*Solanum pseudo-capiscum*	Grown as annual. White blossoms, then orange-red berries that last all winter. 1–2 feet.	Sun at least 4 hours a day.	Warm: 68–72. Cooler at night.
Kafir Lily	*Clivia miniata*	Dark green strap leaves. Cluster of orange lilylike blossoms on 12–15 inch stalks. Buy potted plant.	Bright, indirect light.	Hot: 70 and higher. Cooler at night.
Kalanchoe	*K. blossfeldiana*	Green waxy leaves, flowers red or yellow for Christmas if given 14 hours of darkness from September to October.	South window, sun at least 4 hours a day.	Warm: 68–72. Cooler at night.
Kentia Palm	*Howeia forsteriana*	Feather-shaped foliage; long, narrow leaflets. Dark green. Very hardy. Single stem; often planted several to one pot. Can be small or tree-sized, 4–6 feet.	Filtered light or an hour or two of angled sunlight.	Will take cool, 50, or warm, 60–70.

(*Degrees Fahrenheit)

HUMIDITY	WATERING	FEEDING
Needs humidity. Keep soil moist.	Water generously.	Feed once a month.
All geraniums: Avoid dry air. Set pots on stones with water under them.	All geraniums: Don't water until soil is dry. Then water generously.	All geraniums: Feed every 2 weeks, half strength.
Needs humidity. Keep soil moist.	Daily.	Fertilize monthly.
Needs humidity.	Water each morning. Let it get more dry when bloom is gone.	Do not fertilize.
Not too humid.	Water generously, but let soil dry out between watering.	Very little feeding or foliage will take over from bloom.
Not too humid.	Same as Impatiens.	Same as Impatiens.
Not necessary.	Moderate watering. Let soil dry out between waterings.	Ever. 2 months, half-strength fertilizer.
Likes humidity.	Soak thoroughly, then let it become nearly dry before watering again.	Feed mild solution of fertilizer every month.
Needs humidity.	Water thoroughly. Let dry between watering. In fall, hold back water.	Fertilize every month until fall, then stop until mid-December.
Likes dry soil.	Soak soil thoroughly, then let it become nearly dry before watering again.	Feed mild solution of fertilizer every week.
Soil should stay moist.	Daily. But plant can go without water for several days.	Once a month during spring and early summer while plant is growing.

House Plants *(Continued)*

Common Name	Horticultural	Description and Cultural Suggestions	Light	Temperature*
Lady Palm	*Rhapsis excelsa*	Fan-shaped leaf, deep green. Young plants more beautiful. Grows slowly; 3–4 feet.	Light shade. No sun.	Moderately warm: 65.
Lavender	*Lavendula spica*	Beautiful plant; blue flower. Dries for making sachets for linen closets.	Full sun.	Warm: 60–70.
Lobelia	*L. erinus*	Buy potted plants in spring. They will bloom all spring and summer, even in fall if you cut back seed. Put 3 or 4 plants in 4-inch clay pots. Many varieties, blue best.	Indirect light, partial sun.	Warm: 60–80. at night.
Madagascar Jasmine	*Stephanotis floribunda*	Vine. Deep green; white flowers, fragrance of orange blossoms. Give trellis, in pot, on which to climb.	South window, 4 hours sun.	Warm: 70 or higher. Cooler at night.
Narcissus	*N.* hybrids	Many varieties. Study catalogs. Buy in bud or bloom, or force in September or October. Don't cut foliage until it turns yellow. Plant bulbs outdoors that summer.	Bright indirect light.	Cool: 65–68. Cooler at night.
Oleander	*Nerium oleander*	Evergreen shrub, 2–5 feet. Flowers pink, red, white, purple; November to May. Put on sun porch or outdoors in summer if possible. Juice from stems and foliage poisonous.	Full sun.	Warm: 65–70.
Parsley	*Petroselinum crispum*	Buy pots for kitchen windowsill. Difficult to seed.	Full sun.	Warm: 60–70.
Patent Leather Flower	*Anthurium scherzerianum*	Plant about 12 inches; leaves 6 inches, leathery. Flowers orange, red, pink, spotted white. Buy potted plants either in soil or osmunda.	Bright, indirect light. West window.	Hot: 65–80.
Pepper Plant	*Capsicum annuum*	Buy when white flowers show, then watch peppers develop. Change color as they ripen: green, white, yellow, red, purple. Tree about 12 inches high.	Likes 4 hours direct sun. Put in south window.	Warm: 65–70.
Petunia	*P. hybrida*	Single, double, hanging varieties. Buy potted plants in spring, or dig up old plants in fall, cut back and take in for winter bloom. All colors.	South window, 4 hours sun each day.	Warm: 68–72. Cooler at night.
Philodendron	*P. selloum*	Stout treelike stem. Leaves 18–28 inches. Spathe, hooded at top, is green but bordered white. Dark green leathery leaves are deeply cut in young plants. Can grow to 6 feet tall or be only 1½ feet high.	Doesn't like sun; medium light.	Warm: 65–70.
Philodendron, Heartleaf	*P. oxycardium*	A hardy, heart-shaped green vine. It will grow in clear water or in a pot of humusy soil. Put a wire above it to frame a window. It will climb on a neon stick.	No sun; will take shaded light or live away from a window.	Warm: 65–70.
Pineapple Lily	*Eucomis undulata*	South African bulb. Pot in 7-inch pot. Dark green lancelike foliage. Flower tall, white, about 28 inches high. Lasts 6 weeks.	Sunny window.	Warm: 65–75.

150

*(*Degrees Fahrenheit)*

HUMIDITY	WATERING	FEEDING
Soil should stay moist.	Water each morning.	Once a month, half strength.
Likes to be dry.	Daily.	Fertilize once a month, half strength.
Not necessary.	Daily.	Fertilize about every 2 weeks with low nitrogen but high potash and phosphorous contents: 15–30–30.
Needs humidity.	Daily while it's growing. Drier in winter.	Feed monthly from March to October.
Needs humidity.	Water generously.	Do not fertilize.
Likes humidity.	Water generously, except in dark winter months.	Once or twice a month, March to October.
Needs humidity.	Daily.	Fertilize once a month, half strength.
Soil moist all the time. Set in tray of damp pebbles.	Daily, for soil or osmunda.	Feed sparingly, one-half strength if planted in soil. Don't feed at all if planted in osmunda.
Likes humidity.	Daily. Keep soil moist.	Do not fertilize.
Not necessary.	Water thoroughly each day, but be sure ground dries out between watering.	Fertilize about every 2 weeks with water-soluble fertilizer.
Likes moist air.	Every other day. Let soil dry between waterings.	Three times a year.
Likes moisture.	Every other day. Let soil dry between waterings.	Three times a year.
Needs humidity.	Water generously each day.	Feed every 2 weeks.

House Plants *(Continued)*

COMMON NAME	HORTICULTURAL	DESCRIPTION AND CULTURAL SUGGESTIONS	LIGHT	TEMPERATURE*
Pocketbook Flower	*Calceolaria crenatiflora*	Best to get plants from florist. Spring bloom, fat pouches of red, pink, maroon, yellow with brown or purple dots. Lasts about month.	Bright light, no sun.	Cool: 60.
Podocarpus	*P. marcrophylla maki*	Compact, dark green thin-leaved shrub or tree. Slow growing; 9 inches to 3 feet.	Takes sun or shade.	Likes cool temperature.
Poet's Jasmine	*Jasminum officinale*	Vine. Blooms June to October. Star-shaped fragrant blossom. Give trellis to climb.	Sun 4 hours daily.	Warm: 68–72. Cooler at night.
Poinsettia	*Euphorbia pulcherrima*	Bracts supply color: pink, red, white. Buy plants.	Sunny window at least 4 hours a day.	Warm: 65–70.
Rosemary	*Rosmarinus officinalis*	Evergreen. Beautiful shrub. Blue flower. Take only leaves for cooking to save shrub.	Full sun.	Warm: 60–70.
Rubber Plant	*Ficus elastica*	Evergreen shrub or tree. Glossy green leaves, red-tinted on reverse. From 1½ to 12 feet. Very hardy.	Any exposure. Can grow away from window.	Will stand 60–75.
Schefflera	*S. actinophylla*	Shrub or potted tree. Ordinary soil. Shiny leaves.	Medium light.	Cool or warm: 60–75.
Shrimp Plant	*Beloperone guttata*	Tiny white flowers, but name comes from bracts shaped like shrimp. Red, yellow. Blooms all year.	South window, sun 4 hours a day.	Warm: 68–72. Cooler at night.
Sweet Olive	*Osmanthus fragrans*	Leathery, dark green leaves; white small flowers, fragrance like orange blossoms. 2–3 feet tall. Blooms all year.	Bright sun or light shade. East window in summer.	warm: 68–72. Cooler at night.
Tarragon	*Artemisia dracunculus*	Perennial. Good soil. 12 inches tall in pot.	Light shade. Bright light. No direct sun.	Cool: 60–70.
Thyme, English	*Thymus vulgaris*	Light, sandy soil. 6–8 inches.	Sun, south or south-east window.	Cool: 65–70.
Thyme, Lemon	*Thymus serpyllum citriodorus*	Sandy soil. 6–8 inches.	Sun, south or south-east window.	Cool: 65–70.
Tulip	*Tulipa* hybrids	Many categories, all colors. Study catalogs. Size from 4 inches to 3 feet. Don't save bulbs because they will not bloom again outside.	Bright indirect light.	Warm: 68. Cooler at night.
Watermelon Begonia	*Peperomia sandersi argyreia*	Blue-green leaves with silvery bands.	Shade, no sun.	Warm: 65–70.
Weeping Fig	*Ficus benjamina*	Compact tree, drooping branches, pointed oval leaves. Slow growth; 6 or 7 feet high.	Little light. Does not need to be near window.	Cool. 60–70.

152

*(*Degrees Fahrenheit)*

HUMIDITY	WATERING	FEEDING
Doesn't need humidity.	Water *Calceolaria* carefully so that you don't wet the crowns of the foliage at soil level. Keep soil barely moist so it will be dry by evening.	Do not fertilize when plant is blossoming.
Needs humidity.	Daily, so that it is evenly moist. Don't ever let the soil become dry.	Fertilize twice a year with mild soluble fertilizer.
Needs humidity.	Daily.	Fertilize every 2 weeks.
Let pot sit on pebbles to prevent dryness.	Water thoroughly, but let soil dry between waterings.	No fertilizer when blooming.
Soil should not be wet.	Daily.	Fertilize once a month, half strength.
Not necessary.	Water thoroughly, then let dry completely before watering again.	Once every 6 months give half-strength fertilizer.
Likes humidity.	Moderate. Let dry between waterings.	Mild feeding every 2 months.
Not necessary.	Each morning. Let soil dry between waterings.	Every 2 weeks.
Soil should be moist.	Daily.	Feed every month.
Not necessary.	Daily.	Mild feeding once a month.
Not necessary.	Daily.	Every 2 weeks.
Not necessary.	Daily.	Every 2 weeks.
Needs humidity. Soil moist.	Water generously.	Do not fertilize.
Not necessary.	Do not water too much. Let soil become completely dry, then set pot into saucer of water till top is wet again.	Every 4 months, half-strength feeding.
Not necessary.	Moderate. Let soil dry between waterrngs.	Feed every 6 months.

Hanging Plants

COMMON NAME	HORTICULTURAL	DESCRIPTION AND CULTURAL SUGGESTIONS	LIGHT
Achimenes	*A. hybrida*	In the South. 8–12 inches high, leaves and and twigs spreading. Colors: blue, pink, purple, yellow. After flowering spring and summer it dies down. In October take basket down; store in cool, dark room until February when it shows green growth again.	Bright, indirect light or filtered sunlight.
Begonia, Hanging 'Aphrodite Rose'	Cultivar of Rieger's Elatior *Begonia*	Double rose blossom resulting from exposure of 'Aphrodite Rose' to gamma rays and fast neutrons at Oak Ridge, Tennessee. Compact dark green foliage; blooms 10 months a year. Disease-resistant.	No direct sun. Bright filtered light.
Begonia, Tuberous (for basket)	*B. tuberhybrida pendula*	Grow from tubers or buy plant in basket from florist. Red, pink, yellow, white, salmon.	No direct sun, but bright filtered light. West window, November–March.
Bougainvillea	*B. glabra*	Tropical plant that does well in basket. Red, rose, orange, pink. Color comes from bracts. Often rests in fall and winter.	South window, full sun.
Browallia	*B. speciosa major*	White or blue. Blooms all year. 12–18 inches. Good garden soil.	Filtered sun.
Burro-Tailed Sedum	*Sedum morganianum*	Succulent. Trailing stems 3–4 feet long. Thick gray-green tuberlike leaves overlapping. Keep out of drafts.	Filtered sun or bright light.
Button Fern	*Pellaea rotundifolia*	A small, graceful fern. Round, dark leaflets on hairy stems.	East window, filtered light.
Episcia 'Acajou'	*Episcia*	Silvery green leaf with mahogany border. Red flowers. At end of summer discard plant; buy another in fall. Hang near window.	Full sun in winter. In spring, bright light or part shade.
Fuchsia Hybrid	*Fuchsia*	Single or double bloom. Marvelous colors: pink and lavender, rose and white, blue and crimson. Good soil plus bonemeal.	Bright filtered light, not sun. East or west window.
Geranium Ginger	*Pelargonium*	Small round, toothed leaves. Lavender bloom. Sweet scent.	Sun 4 hours per day.
Ivy	*Pelargonium peltatum*	Trails 2–3 feet. Glossy, bright green ivylike leaves with pointed lobes. White, pink, red, rose, lavender in rounded clusters. Remove faded blooms. Pinch to make more bushy.	Sunny window; as much light as possible.
Lemon Crispum	*Pelargonium crispum*	Leaves small, ruffled. Blooms pink, Lemon fragrance.	Sun 4 hours per day.
Nutmeg Variegated	*Pelargonium fragrans*	Green and white leaves; fragrance like nutmeg.	Sun 4 hours per day.

TEMPERATURE*	HUMIDITY	WATERING	FEEDING
Hot: 70–75. Cooler at night: 65–70.	Likes humidity.	Water generously until flowers are gone, then reduce water. In February, when new life shows, water it again.	Fertilize every 2 weeks with food marked 15–30–15.
Needs heat during day: 68–70. Cool at night: 55–60.	Keep soil moist.	Water heavily on bright days, not so much on dark days.	When growing well, fertilize with 10–10–5 soluble every 2 weeks. Or use fishmeal every 2 weeks.
Needs heat during day: 68–70. Cool at night: 55–60.	Keep soil moist.	Water heavily on bright days, not so much on dark days.	When growing well, fertilize with 10–10–5 soluble every 2 weeks. Or use fishmeal every two weeks.
Hot: 70–75. Cooler at night.	Not necessary.	Water thoroughly. Let soil dry between waterings. Reduce water when plant is resting.	Fertilize every 2 weeks when plant is blooming. Don't feed when resting.
Warm: 70–72.	Likes moist soil.	Daily.	Fertilize every 2 weeks, half strength.
Hot: 65–75.	Keep soil evenly moist, except in winter. Then it can become quite dry.	Daily, except in winter.	Fertilize 2 or 3 times each season, half strength.
Warm: 65–72.	As much humidity as possible. Let pot sit on pebbles if it is in a solid container.	Daily.	Fertilize every month.
Hot: 75. Cooler at night: 65–70.	Needs humidity. Keep soil moist. Put pot on pebbles, if possible, to give water below the roots.	Water generously.	Fertilize once a month while plant is growing and blooming.
Warm: 60–70. Cooler at night.	Don't let soil get dry. Sun porch or terrace good for humidity, if possible.	Daily. Soil should be evenly moist.	Fertilize each week with fishmeal, one-third less than usual dosage.
Warm: 65–75. Cooler at night.	Likes humidity.	Water thoroughly. Let soil dry out between waterings.	Fertilize every 2 weeks from March to October. After that, once a month.
Warm: 65–75. Cooler at night.	Likes humidity.	Water generously. Let soil dry out between waterings.	Fertilize half strength every 2 weeks from March to October. After that, once a month.
Warm: 65–75. Cooler at night.	Likes humidity.	Water generously. Let soil dry out between waterings.	Fertilize half strength, every 2 weeks from March to October. After that, once a month.
Warm: 65–75. Cooler at night.	Likes humidity.	Water thoroughly when needs it. Let soil dry out between waterings.	Fertilize every 2 weeks from March to October. After that, once a month.

*(*Degrees Fahrenheit)*

Hanging Plants *(Continued)*

COMMON NAME	HORTICULTURAL	DESCRIPTION AND CULTURAL SUGGESTIONS	LIGHT
Geranium Rose	*Pelargonium graveolens*	Deeply cut leaves, lavender bloom. Leaves scented like roses.	Sun 4 hours per day. South window.
Jasmine (Royal Jasmine or Angelwing Jasmine)	*Jasminum gracilis magnificum*	Clusters of white star-shaped blossoms. Very fragrant in winter.	Sun 4 hours per day.
Kangaroo Vine	*Cissus antarctica*	Hardy, "tough" green vine. Grows slowly. Leaves shaped like elm leaves, jagged edge. Graceful line over basket.	Doesn't require light from window. Content in center of room.
Lantana	*L. montevidensis*	Trailing vine. Rosy-lavender blooms. Sandy soil. Buy potted plant. Cut back to control shape.	Full sun in winter, 4 hours per day.
Nasturtium 'Semi-Tall Double Gleam'	*Tropaeolum majus*	Trailing, fragrant blooming vine. Hardy, easy to grow. Can climb small wire lattice or trail over edge of basket.	South window. Sun 4 hours per day.
Orchid	*Cymbidium* hybrids terrestrial (soil)	Buy potted plant near blooming age. "Soil" is mixture of osmunda fiber, coarse peat moss, and leaf mold. Hang on sun porch or in window.	Medium light; 3 hours bright sun per day plus 5 hours daylight.
	Dendrobium nobile: epiphytic (air plant)	Buy plant near blooming age, strapped or wired to slab of cork or tree fern with roots covered with pad of osmunda. Hook in window or on sun porch.	Bright light: 5 hours sun per day plus 5 hours under lights after sunset.
	Phalaenopsis lindeni: terrestial (soil)	Buy plant potted, near blooming age. Plastic pot slashed on sides for drainage. Place in basket on sun porch or window.	Shade: bright sun 3 hours per day or 16 hours on growth lights 6 inches below.
Petunia 'White Cascade'	*P. hybrida grandiflora*	Large-flowered white blossom. 15 inches high. Trailing for boxes and baskets. Buy started plants. Pick off seeds and dead blossoms.	Sun, south or west window.
Spider Plant	*Chlorophytum elatum*	Long green blades of foliage with little white blossoms and roots at their tips. Can be planted for more hanging spider plants. Hardy. Fast-growing.	East light, filtered sun.
Wandering Jew	*Tradescantia fluminensis*	Dark green leaves or light green striped with yellow or white. Long trailing stems. Hardy. Fast grower.	Good light: sun.
	Zebrina pendula	Purplish green leaves with bands of pink, white, red. Long trailing vine. Hardy.	Good light: sun.
Wax Plant	*Hoya carnosa*	Red-stemmed vine with green leaves that are thick and look as if made of wax. Will climb or grow over edge of basket. Flowers pink, purple eye; fragrant. Takes couple of years to bloom, then flowers constantly. Don't cut back stem; that's where flowers appear.	Sun or bright indirect light or filtered light.

Temperature*	Humidity	Watering	Feeding
Warm: 65–75. Cooler at night.	Likes humidity.	Water generously. Let soil dry out between waterings.	Fertilize half strength every 2 weeks from March to October. After that, once a month.
Warm: 70–72. Cooler at night.	Keep soil moist.	Daily.	Fertilize every 2 weeks except when plant is resting.
Cool: 55–65.	Keep soil moist but not too wet.	Daily.	Fertilize every 6 months.
Warm: 68–72. Cooler at night.	Not necessary.	Water thoroughly. Let soil dry out between waterings.	Fertilize every 2 weeks, half strength.
Warm: 60–68. Cooler at night.	Keep soil moist.	Daily.	Fertilize every month with food that has more phosphorus and potash in it than nitrogen to keep blossoms coming.
Cool: 68 or higher by day. Night: 50–60.	Likes humidity. Mist every day except when in bud or flower. Set on wet pebbles.	Water carefully each morning. When plant flowers, don't water.	High nitrogen fertilizer (20–10–10) diluted to quarter strength, every week. Every 3 months water with an organic soluble fertilizer.
Cool. Winter: 60–70 day, 50–60 night.	Same as *Cymbidium*.	Same as *Cymbidium*.	Same as *Cymbidium*.
Warm: 70–80. Cooler at Night: 60–70.	Same as *Cymbidium*.	Same as *Cymbidium*.	Same as *Cymbidium*.
Warm: 68–72. Cooler at night.	Needs humidity.	Water generously. Let soil dry out between waterings.	Fertilize every 2 weeks.
Warm: 65–70.	Keep humidity high. Soil moist.	Daily.	Fertilize once a month.
Warm: 65–70.	Not necessary.	Water when dry.	Fertilize once a month.
Warm: 65–70.	Not necessary.	Water when dry.	Fertilize once a month.
Warm: 65–70.	Not necessary.	Water generously. Make sure the drainage is good.	Fertilize every 2 months, spring and summer.

(*Degrees Fahrenheit)

157

INDEX*

* Page numbers in boldface indicate pages on which there are illustrations.

ABCDE